Survival! A School Kid's Guide

Do you feel unwell most Monday mornings, but on top of the world on Friday afternoon?

Do your eyes water when it's liver and bacon for lunch but light up when it's sausage and beans?

Are you revolted when your teacher asks you the difference between a toad and an earthworm, but revived when they suggest you might do a nature study in the park for a change?

You do? You *are*?!

Then you had better read SURVIVAL! A SCHOOL KID'S GUIDE – fast!

About the author

GLADYS OVER was once a school kid
but is happy to inform you that she
managed to survive. SURVIVAL!
A SCHOOL KID'S GUIDE is her first
title for Knight Books.

Survival! A School Kid's Guide

Illustrated by
Tony Blundell

Sponsored by Henkel
Chemicals, makers of Pritt

KNIGHT BOOKS
Hodder and Stoughton

British Library C.I.P.

Over, Gladys
Survival!
1. School life – Manuals – For
students
I. Title   II. Blundell, Tony,
1951–
371.8

ISBN 0-340-41422-7

Printed and bound in Great Britain
for Hodder and Stoughton Paper-
backs, a division of Hodder and
Stoughton Ltd., Mill Road, Dunton
Green, Sevenoaks, Kent TN13 2YA.
(Editorial Office: 47 Bedford Square,
London WC1B 3DP) by Cox & Wyman
Ltd., Reading, Berks. Photoset by
Rowland Phototypesetting Limited,
Bury St Edmunds, Suffolk

Contents

The Summer Term 87

Introduction

Whether we like it or not we all have to go to school.
This is called receiving an education, and is meant to
prepare us for the long, hard road of life we have to
travel. At any rate this is what we are told by our
parents and teachers. To those still at school it's more
like an endurance test. Do you realize that if you add up
all the time you spend at school, you would get an
astonishing total of 12,870 hours, in other words 536·25
whole days and nights, or every minute of one and a half
years! And that is the minimum time – it doesn't
include going to nursery school or play school before
the age of five, or staying on in the sixth form after
sixteen.

The people at Pritt, who, unlike a lot of grown-ups,
can remember what it was like to be at school, thought
something was needed to help pupils survive this mam-
moth endurance test, so here it is. It's packed with tips
on how to cope with almost everything you will encounter at school, from your first day to your last. Some hints
are the favourites of various children whose opinions we
canvassed – though some of *their* suggestions were so
outrageous we had to sneak them into the book without
the publisher knowing! Some of the tips are meant to be
taken more seriously than others, but they should all
give food for thought, and for fun.

But that's not all. Each term has a special project for

you to carry out, a selection of terrible classroom clangers, a handful of practical jokes to play on unsuspecting friends a timetable of events for you to fill in, and a few surprises. And what better to help you survive school than a good selection of jokes? You'll find plenty to make you laugh at the foot of nearly every page.

Keep this book by you for the whole of your 12,870 hours. It may become the most useful thing you possess!

Personal Record

First of all, just for the record, fill in this page.

NAME ...... Beth Wilmshurst ......

ADDRESS ...... Tamarinds, 19 HallowHill
ST. Andrews, Fife, Scotland,
KY16 8SF 8SF ......

SCHOOL ...... Strathkinness Primary ......

FORM ...... P.7 ......

FORM TEACHER'S REAL NAME ...... Diann Bennett

FORM TEACHER'S NICKNAME ...... Mrs. B ......

HEAD TEACHER'S NAME ...... Diann Bennett

THE BEST THING ABOUT HIM/HER ...... nothing

....

THE WORST THING ABOUT HIM/HER ....
...... everything ......

FAVOURITE SUBJECT ...... Art ......

MOST HATED SUBJECT ...... Maths ......

9

The Autumn Term

TERM BEGINS ON .... ☹

DATES TO REMEMBER ....

31 October (Hallowe'en) ....

5 November (Guy Fawkes' Day) ....

We break up for half term on ....

We go back after half term on ....

We have our carol concert/Christmas revue on ....

....

We have our Christmas party/Christmas dinner on .....

....

SPECIAL PROJECTS THIS TERM ....

.... the Sea / ~~red~~ coast

.... Japan

....

....

....

EXAM DATES THIS TERM ....

....

....

....

....

....

....

**FRIENDS' AND FAMILY BIRTHDAYS
THIS TERM** ....

.... My birthday ....

...... April 30th wednesday .....

....

....

....

....

....

....

....

....

TERM ENDS ON........................ ☺ (HURRAY!)

13

Autumn is the season of mists and mellow fruitfulness, according to the poet Keats (see the entry under *English*, on page 15). It is also the beginning of the school year, when pupils drag themselves reluctantly back from long summer holidays and teachers try to fill them with good intentions towards achieving magnificent results in all their work. Hmmm. A more cheerful thought is that it is a term with lots of opportunities for celebrations – Hallowe'en, Guy Fawkes' Day, and, of course, Christmas. This section of the book tells you how to make a pop-up card for Christmas and has a useful list of suggestions for presents to make or buy for people you find difficult to please. There is also a section on road safety, there are some amazing classroom clangers, lots of jokes, a space in which you can draw your (un)favourite teacher, and – er – oh yes, a few tips on how to survive some of the things you'll encounter in this first term of a new year.

Assembly

Provided you are not overlooked by a teacher or a prefect or a goody-goody sneak, you can prevent boredom in assembly by taking with you something to read. Or take a piece of paper and a pencil and play noughts and crosses with your neighbour, or some other game (for suggestions, see pages 70–74).

If there is singing in your school assembly and you either hate it or can't sing, then mouth the words energetically. No one will know that the melodic singing drifting round the hall doesn't come partly from you. If other people's singing is particularly bad, invest in a pair of ear plugs. Small malleable wax ear plugs can be bought from a chemist's and are invaluable in shutting out unwanted sounds. (You could also use them to feign deafness in lessons, but be careful not to be caught out or you'll get into trouble.)

A good way to annoy someone you dislike in assembly is to sit behind them and rest your foot/feet on the back of their chair, so you poke them in the bottom. They will hate this but will be unable to turn round and tell you to stop in case they get told off by a teacher.

English

English is probably the most important subject in the whole school curriculum. (This word means the courses of study offered by a school, not something you use to groom a horse.) English lessons are divided into English Language, which means sentence construction, grammar, spelling, writing essays, and so on; and English Literature, which is the study of novels, plays and poetry. You will discover the plays of William Shakespeare, which can cause confusion in history lessons by making you think that King Henry IV was a man divided into two parts; the poetry of Keats, Shelley, Byron, Tennyson, and (if you're lucky) modern writers like Roger McGough too; and Great Works of Literature. These tend to be novels written in the nineteenth century by people like Jane Austen and Thomas Hardy, and you probably won't understand them until you've left school.

People either love English or loathe it. Those who enjoy it like hearing and using words, enjoying reading a good story, and appreciate the lilt and rhythm of poetry. Those who don't, get bored with the fussiness of

Why did Sally Solo stand on a ladder when singing in assembly?

spelling and punctuation, and with things they don't understand in plays and poetry. But whatever your feelings about it, it is a necessary subject, because it is all about communication – a vital part of everyday life. If spelling and punctuation are wrong, then the meaning of the words is often not clear, and communication is not achieved. The best way to improve your English is to read as many books as possible. Read books that are fun as well as those your teachers say you should read, for enjoying reading will help you later to appreciate books that may seem heavy going now.

Look up!

If you think this book is getting a bit too serious, you can now breathe a sigh of relief. Here's a simple trick to try next time you are waiting for a teacher to come into the room.

If possible, get the whole class prepared beforehand, otherwise get as many of the people around you in on the act as you can. Wait until the teacher has come in, then, one by one, until everyone is doing it, look up at the ceiling. Pretend you have seen something amazing there. Study it carefully, and if you dare, tap your neighbour on the shoulder and point ceiling-wards. Your teacher will start to look too, and be puzzled as to what you can all see. This is a very old trick, but it never fails to work, even on teachers who have seen it many times before.

Teachers

Whole volumes could be written about teachers, but I'll try to confine it to a page or two. The first thing to learn about them is that you can never escape them entirely, no matter how clever you are. So you have to learn how to cope with them, and the ways of doing this depend on the teacher in question. They tend to fall into types. Six different types are listed below, and if one of yours doesn't fit into one of these categories, then you'll just have to ask people who've been at the school longer than you the best way to deal with them. Of course, if you want to please your teachers, all you have to do is to work very, very hard, be extra polite, open doors for

TEACHER: What is the Order of the Bath, Samantha?

them, offer to clean the board, carry books, and so on (see *Pets, teachers'*, page 132). But if you merely want to survive them with the minimum of damage being inflicted on you, here are some helpful hints:

1. Are they roundish, fresh-faced, energetic and hearty? (This type is usually, but not always, a games teacher.) They like people who seem energetic, tough, full of common sense and with a sense of humour. They loathe anyone who whines, makes excuses or seems feeble, so if you want to get round them pretend to be the hearty type, even if you're not.

2. Are they stern-looking, with cold blue eyes, a pale face and a lean and hungry look? This is a type to avoid. You will probably have noticed how they can quieten a room just by appearing in the doorway. My advice with

SAMANTHA: Mum, Dad, then me.

this sort is to be polite, try and answer their questions (though you may get away with lurking quietly at the back for a while), and do your best not to antagonize them. If you do happen to cross them, I recommend a hasty and heartfelt prayer, even if you are not normally given to this kind of thing.

3. Are they smiling, kindly, and with a sense of humour? If so, count your blessings, for this type is becoming an endangered species. You may be able to get round this sort's kind heart with a sob story (terribly

sorry, couldn't do my homework because I hurt my wrist/had to spend all evening helping with the housework because my mother's ill/had to spend all evening helping with the baby because my mother, sister and father are all ill, etc.) but don't try it too often. No matter how kind-hearted, he or she is still a teacher.

4. Are they the sarcastic type? It is difficult to know how to handle this sort. They appear to like humour, but if *you* try to be funny they are likely to turn the tables on you so the laugh ends up being at your expense. Treat them with extreme caution – with some of them no matter what you say or do they'll find a way of making you look stupid.

5. Are they young, possibly in their first job, and completely incapable of keeping control of the class? With this kind of teacher you can do virtually as you like, but they make it almost too easy and this rather spoils the fun! Try to resist the temptation to send them up too much, or you may become the last straw in their

lives, and turn them into nervous wrecks. Although it's hard to believe, teachers are people, too.

6. Are they the sort that is a physical turn-off? Men of this kind wear awful ill-fitting clothes, have dandruff and BO; women tend to have ginger moustaches and hairy legs. They are the sort that everyone loves to make fun of, but remember they are human beings and

MATHS TEACHER: If I have five apples in one hand and seven apples in the other, what have I got?

don't be too unkind. Try to be helpful in their lessons and don't giggle behind their backs. They may not be as thick-skinned as they seem, and you should never be cruel to be funny.

Using the lines and squiggles on this page, draw a picture of your favourite (or least favourite) teacher.

susie: Big hands, Miss.

You can make them as attractive, or as horrendous, as you like.

Art

The great thing about art is that it can be fun both for those who are good at it and those who are not. The good ones get pleasure from being able to create wonderful pictures that actually resemble the subject matter, or vivid abstract designs that everyone can see are pretty (even if they don't understand them), while the not-so-good can have fun splashing red paint around and pretending to have cut an artery (art-ery, ho, ho), spotting red paint around and pretending to have got measles, or smearing green paint on their faces and pretending they're going to be sick. They can also have fun painting an abstract picture of the oddest teacher in the school with the weirdest-looking face you've ever seen and calling it Ivan the Terrible or Genghis Khan (you may have practised on the previous page). No one will ever know the difference.

Hockey

There are only two good things about hockey. The first is that it has to be endured for only half the year, and the second is the bully off, which can be fun and is well named, for the game is full of bullies.

Hockey is definitely a game for the athletic. You have to be able to run for miles through the mud, with wind and rain lashing at your bare legs, all for the sake of clobbering a ball with a strangely-shaped bat (sorry, stick). The only way to avoid having to do this is to volunteer to be the goalie, but the trouble with this is that it means standing still and freezing with cold for a large part of the game. And when you get your chance to try and stop the ball, you run the risk of mortal injury, not only from the ball, but from the mêlée of assorted sticks crashing around your shins. This, of course, is a hazard of playing hockey, for big beefy players with reddened hefty legs are always pushing in with their sticks where they're not wanted. You can, of course, try batting them one with your stick, but this can get out of hand and if they retaliate you will come off worse. The best ploy is to loiter palely at the edge of the action, pretending to be playing the game and making the odd dash up and down to keep warm, but making sure your precious pins are well out of reach of flailing sticks.

If you really can't bear playing at all, then the only thing to do is to forge a medical certificate saying that your knees/ankles/nerves are so weak that you are excused hockey.

School dinners

> If you stay to school dinners
> Better throw them aside;
> A lot of kids didn't,
> A lot of kids died.
> The meat is made of iron,
> The spuds are made of steel.
> If that don't get you
> The afters will.

There can hardly be a pupil in the land who will not agree with that verse, except perhaps those who've never had school dinners. (If that includes you, don't feel deprived, you're one of the lucky ones!)

A recent survey put fish and chips, fish fingers and chips, roast meat, and sausage and chips at the top of the favourite school dinners list, with ice-cream, cake, apple pie, and yogurt heading the puddings. The most hated school dinners were, for the main course, salad, fish or fish fingers (!), cheese pie, stew, and liver, and the most hated puddings were rice, semolina, and sponge puddings other than chocolate. Lots of people also hated potatoes, cabbage, peas, and custard. How do your tastes compare with these?

The only tip for surviving school dinners if you have to have them is to take a doggy bag to hide the horrid bits in. But don't make the mistake of leaving the cheese pie or liver and then being so hungry that you eat three helpings of the pudding, especially if it is an unpopular one such as prunes, (if it is a popular one you won't get even a second helping) because you will spend an uncomfortable evening if you do.

You may, of course, take a packed lunch to school. If so, and no matter how much you like crisps, chips, sweet things and cakes, make sure it contains either meat, cheese or eggs, and salad vegetables and fresh fruit. Wholemeal bread is better for you than white bread, too. If you try and eat these things, together with fresh vegetables when you have a cooked meal, and drink water rather than lots of fizzy drinks and tea and coffee, you will stay healthier and look better, too, with a clear, fresh skin and shiny hair.

Classroom clangers

Each term has a selection of classic clangers, taken from the exercise books and examination papers of pupils who prefer to remain anonymous. Here are some from English books and papers:

We were shown onto the aeroplane by a nice lady called a hostage.

Poetry is when every line starts with a capital letter.

The wife of a duke is called a ducky.

The bowels are a, e, i, o and u.

Hansel was a little boy in a fairy tale. He had a sister called Gristle.

A man who makes spectacles is called an optimist.

Then, without a word of warning, the sheep all ran across the road.

An epitaph is a short sarcastic poem.

People who live in Moscow are called mosquitoes.

Shakespeare wrote tragedy, comedy and errors.

Polonius was a sort of sausage.

And here are some from French:

'Silver plate' is French for 'please'.

'Monsoon' is French for 'mister'.

The French call their national anthem 'The Mayonnaise'.

GEOGRAPHY TEACHER: Where are the Andes?

And some from geography:

In High Wycombe they make furniture from beaches in the Chilterns.

The horizon is a line where the land meets the sky, but it isn't there when you get there.

Manilla is a city famous for its envelopes.

The Sewage Canal lies between Africa and the Middle East.

A fjord is a Norwegian car.

And finally, some from science:

Volts are named after Voltaire, who invented electricity.

Gravity is something that if it didn't exist we would all fly away.

SIMPLE SIMON: At the end of my armies.

Margarine is made from imitation cows.

A ruminating animal is one that chews its cubs.

Geography

As Edmund Clerihew Bentley* said, 'Biography is about chaps, geography is about maps.' (Actually he said it the other way round but it makes more sense here this way round.) Geography *is* about maps, so whatever you do, don't get lost on your way to the geography classroom or everyone will think you're a real wally.

You will be expected to remember lots of things about maps and towns and rivers and mountains for geography, so here are a few to give you a head start. The Arctic is the bit round the North Pole and is all frozen sea; the Antarctic is the bit around the South Pole and is land under all that ice. Penguins live in the Antarctic; polar bears in the Arctic. Or is it the other way round? The longest river in the world is the Nile; the longest river in Great Britain is the Severn. Birmingham is north of London but south of Manchester. Southampton is on the River Itchen, and there really is a place in Dorset called Piddletrenthide. The tallest mountain in Great Britain is Ben Nevis and it is in Scotland. Dundee, also in Scotland, is known for making jute and jam. Redditch, near Birmingham, makes needles and pins, and Northampton makes shoes.

* Ask your English teacher who he is. You see, English crops up again and again, there's no getting away from it.

MRS SMITH: What position does your son play in the school football team?

When you're reading a map, remember that the green bits mean woodland, dotted grey bits mean a park or ornamental grounds, a cross on a circle means a church with a spire and a cross on a rectangle means a church with a tower, and a dotted red line means a public footpath. (This is also useful to remember if you ever go on hikes with friends.) Got all that? Right, you should now be able to face your geography lessons.

Reading

If you have a copy of this book in front of you then presumably you can read. But how fast do you read? The late President Kennedy was said to be able to read four newspapers in twenty minutes – which means reading at a phenomenal rate. It would be handy before exams, wouldn't it? The secret of being able to read fast is for the eye to recognise groups of words rather than individual words. It is a very useful gift, but it does tend to rob reading of much of its pleasure.

Football

Rugby

Rugby has been snobbishly defined as a game for hooligans played by gentlemen, as opposed to soccer, which is said to be a game for gentlemen played by hooligans. You can see what they mean, though – if football (i.e. soccer) is tough, fast and mud-bespattered, rugby is the same only more so.

The game is said to have been born in 1823 when a

MRS JONES: I think he's one of the drawbacks.

30

boy called William Webb Ellis picked up the ball in a football game at Rugby School and ran with it. You can still pick up the ball and run with it today, but then you have to be prepared for some hefty great lout to jump on you and wrest it from your grasp. If you are not careful you end up with a faceful of mud while he goes off with the ball.

It's a great game for licensed hooliganism and for those who like physical contact, but it's not for the faint-hearted. Ask your parents if you are insured before you play, and don't be surprised if your mother gets less and less enthusiastic about washing your kit. The best way to survive rugby is not to indulge in it.

Soccer

Soccer is the most popular game in the world and has almost become a religion for some men. It's a very old game – a type of football was played in England in the Middle Ages – and the rules of the game as we know it were drawn up in the 1800s.

Most of what is written above about rugby applies to soccer, except that it seems to have been devised for people with injured or no arms, as you are allowed to touch the ball with any part of your body except the hands and arms. So it's no use saying you have a sprained wrist and expecting to be let off playing.

Shopping list

Here's a little trick to play on someone who is kind enough to offer to get you some things from the shops while they are going there. Thank them very much, give them a folded list, and say you'll give them the money when they return. When your victim reaches the shop he or she will open the list and start to look for the items on it. But they won't be able to find any of them! The kinds of things you will put on your list are these:

> a bottle of white ink
> a left-handed pencil
> some black blotting paper
> a packet of hot vanilla ice-cream
> a litre of blue-and-white striped paint
> a dozen sheep's eggs

Prefects

Nearly all prefects are horrible. One way to cope with them is to keep out of their way as much as possible – with luck, if you are at a big school, they won't even know your name. If you are unfortunate enough, or unwise enough, to allow your name to be circulated among prefects, then you must be very, very careful. For once they realize that you are a potential source of trouble, they will keep an eye on you and pounce when you least expect it. Some are such bullies they may even try and blame you for things you haven't done, and they are more likely to be believed than you. So if you can't hide from them, or give them a false name (and this will only work in a *very* big school, and then not for long), try practising your sprinting to get as far away as possible in the shortest possible time.

Biology

The first thing to remember when you start biology lessons is that spirogyra is not a Greek dancer, but a freshwater alga about which you will learn quite a lot (and still fail to see its significance in the great order of things). The second thing to remember is to make sure there's a bucket handy in case someone is taken ill when you have to look at some particularly repulsive specimen. Learning about plants and how to draw them can be fun, but remember to sort out the stamens from the anthers and filaments or your drawing won't be appreciated. Ask if you can perform growing experiments and try growing alfalfa sprouts or fenugreek, because then you can eat them with your lunch. When you get older and start to study mammals, in particular the domestic habits of the rabbit, you may well find it a) fascinating and b) an excuse for a bit of a giggle.

TEACHER: Sammy, name three things that contain milk.

Road safety

You may think that advice on road safety is something only very young children need, but you would be wrong. Nowadays there is more traffic than ever on the roads, and drivers are often impatient and in a hurry. We *all* (including teachers) need to brush up on our road safety to try and cut down the number of accidents that occur each year.

Here is the Green Cross Code, which everyone, young and old, should know off by heart and practise every time they are out in the street:

First find a safe place to cross, then stop. Safe places are pedestrian crossings, subways, bridges, traffic lights, where there are islands in the middle of the road, and where a policeman, school crossing patrol or traffic warden is controlling the traffic. If there are none of these, take care not to wait near a bend or near parked vehicles that may obstruct your view.

Stand on the pavement near the kerb. Stand slightly back from the edge of the road, where drivers can see you and where you can see oncoming traffic from both sides.

Look all round for traffic and listen.

If traffic is coming, let it pass. Look all round again.

When there is no traffic near, walk straight across the road.

sᴀᴍᴍʏ: Cheese, ice-cream and three cows.

Keep looking and listening for traffic while you cross.

But that's not all. Remember, if you lark about near a busy road, pushing one another around, or if you suddenly run across a road, or run out from behind a parked vehicle, or leap off a bus (all things you should never do), a driver may not have time to stop or avoid you. Cars take 23 metres to stop when travelling at 30 mph (48 kph), and 53 metres when travelling at 50 mph (80 kph). For this reason, never be tempted to fool around when crossing a road as some teenagers do, it is a very silly and dangerous practice.

If you are out in the dark, wear something light coloured so you can be seen.

If you are riding a bicycle, wear a reflecting belt and armband. (For further information about bicycles, see page 99.)

If you are in charge of a younger child, hold it by the hand and keep it on the inside (i.e. away from the road side) of you. Don't let it run across the road, or it may fall.

If you are in charge of a dog, keep it on a lead at all times when on or near roads, and again, keep it on your inside.

If you are riding a pony, give hand signals in plenty of time. Wear reflective clothing in gloomy weather conditions. Always thank drivers who are courteous. Never take a pony out on the road unless you know it is good in traffic and that you are capable of controlling it.

THIS TERM'S PROJECT

A pop-up Christmas card

Now you can make your very own pop-up cards! If you start early enough, you could make one for each member of your family, and for your closest friends. With a different picture, the card could be adapted for use as a birthday card or a valentine card.

You will need:
1 piece of card 22 cm × 18 cm
2 pieces of card 18 cm × 10 cm
Pritt Multi-Glue
Pritt Stick
pencil
ruler
scissors
crayons, paints, or pictures from old Christmas cards

1. Find the centre points at the top and bottom of the larger piece of card by measuring along its length.

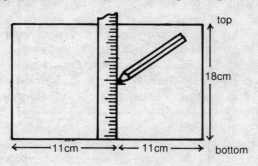

Mark both points, then join them with a lightly drawn pencil line.

2. Measure 7 cm from the bottom of the card along the line you have drawn and draw a short horizontal line at this point. Then measure 3 cm below the horizontal line (i.e. 4 cm from the bottom of the card) and draw another short horizontal line. This marked side will be the inside of your card.

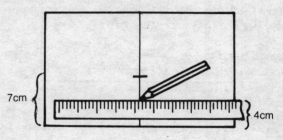

3. Place the ruler along the vertical line you drew first and score lightly along it with the blunt side of the scissors' tip. *Do not cut through it.*

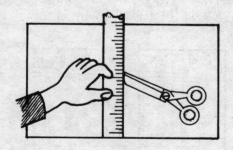

4. Turn the card over, making sure that the bottom of the card is still the area where the short horizontal lines are. On the right-hand half of this card draw and paint a picture of Santa Claus driving his reindeer

sleigh through the skies and snow. (If you can't draw, then find a picture of a suitable size from an old Christmas card, cut it out and stick it down with Pritt Stick.)

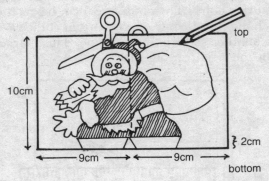

5. Take one of the smaller pieces of card and lightly draw a pencil line down the centre. Draw a picture of Santa with his sack bulging with wonderful presents, centred on the line, and leave 2 cm at the bottom of your picture to make a flap. Colour in the picture and cut it out. (Again, you could use a cut-out picture from another card for this but make sure it will fit onto your smaller piece of card.)

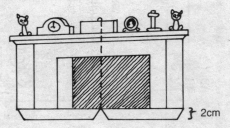

6. Take the other smaller piece of card and lightly draw a pencil line down the centre. Draw a background picture of your living-room, with your fireplace, if you

have one, in the centre. Leave 2 cm at the bottom of your picture to make a flap. Colour in the picture and cut it out. This is to be a background for Santa.

7. Fold back the flaps on your pictures, and fold the pictures in half down the central lines to make a crease. Spread the underside of the flaps with Pritt Multi-Glue.

8. Take the larger piece of card again and open it up. Glue the background picture on the line 7 cm from the bottom of the card, and the Santa picture on the lower line. Make sure the centres of the pictures and the centre of the card all match. Press them down firmly and leave until the glue is quite dry.

7cm — — — —
4cm — — —

9. Carefully fold the card to close it, and open it up again. Santa will spring into life in the centre of your

living-room! All you have to do now is to write a message on the back of the card, and the lucky person who receives it will have a wonderful Christmas surprise.

Alarm (fire)

Schools never have fire drills on warm sunny days when you would like to have an excuse to be outside. Instead they seem to choose cold and often wet days, when you

ALAN: A plate of sausage and chips, please, Sir!

have to stand shivering in the playground until you have all been accounted for. There is a great temptation not to bother going outside but to stay in, in the warm. However, just in case the warmth becomes a bit more than you bargained for (i.e. in case there really is a fire), it is better not to ignore fire alarms, and to troop bravely outside with the rest. If your spies can find out when the drill will be held, then you could conveniently arrange to have your coat and gloves with you in the classroom.

Woodwork

If you want to keep in with the woodwork master then don't use a chisel as a screwdriver. This is guaranteed to turn him against you. Also try not to cut or saw off your own or anyone else's fingers. It makes such a mess, and the woodwork master won't like that either.

Sharpening tools can be a great mystery. You are supposed to hold them at just the right angle, to do this and to do that, and somehow it just doesn't work unless you are one of those who *knows*. Try to get someone to help you if you have to sharpen your tools, or you may spend every carpentry lesson grinding away at the oilstone!

Homework

No matter how strong the temptation, don't copy your homework out of a textbook, or out of anyone else's exercise book. You are bound to be found out and the

SCIENCE TEACHER: If we breathe oxygen in the daytime, what do we breathe at night?

consequences will not be pleasant! If you can't get out of doing homework (and it is difficult to find a consistently foolproof way) then there are two ways of tackling it. The first is to do it as soon as you get home and therefore have the rest of the evening or weekend in which to enjoy yourself; the second is to leave it until the last possible minute, i.e. just before bedtime or on Sunday evening. If you have brothers and sisters it may be possible to bribe them to do your homework for you, or to do a swap if their homework is more to your liking than yours, and vice versa. For excuses about not doing homework see page 106.

Graffiti

No matter how strong the temptation, do not write graffiti on walls. It is unsightly and means spending a lot of time and money cleaning it off again. If your urge to write on walls is absolutely irresistible, then pin a large sheet of paper on your bedroom wall and write on that instead. This can be a lot more fun anyway, as you can invite each friend who visits you to contribute something of their own.

Christmas party trick

Take a balloon – you've probably got one among your Christmas decorations – and blow some air into it, but do not tie the neck. Instead, let the air out very slowly, pulling at the neck as you do so. The balloon will make some very strange noises indeed! Before you play this trick, practise it a few times, for you will discover that the balloon can make different noises, according to how fast you let the air out. When you know you can produce the desired effect, hold the balloon behind your back and make the funny noises at your Christmas party or during the last lesson of the term.

Feeding birds in Winter

You can help wild birds survive the winter (when natural food supplies are scarce) by providing them with suitable additional food. If you are keen on nature study you may be able to persuade your teachers to let you create a bird-feeding area outside where you can all see it. Maybe someone can even make a bird table in a woodwork lesson!

Make sure the place is out of the reach of cats. Whether you have a bird table or not, put some food on the ground, for some birds, such as thrushes, prefer to feed there.

Half a coconut, hung open end downwards, or *unsalted* peanuts in wire mesh containers will attract tits; cheese or fat smeared on tree bark will attract them too, as well as woodpeckers and nuthatches. Insect-eating birds will appreciate little piles of grated cheese among dead leaves and twigs on the ground.

Feed the birds on any of the following (you could bring some of them with you to school): moistened bread or cake, bacon rind and fat, unsalted peanuts, pastry, nuts, fruit, cheese, cooked rice or potato, meal-worms, oatmeal, cat or dog food, and the special mixtures sold for bird-feeding. *Never* feed salted peanuts, desiccated coconut, uncooked rice or dry bread, as these can be harmful.

Move the feeding ground once or twice during the winter to lessen the chance of disease in the birds. Feed

them, if you can, either first thing in the morning or late in the afternoon, to help them live through cold winter nights. Try to arrange for someone who lives near the school to come in and feed them during the holidays.

Birds need water, too. Many die of thirst in winter when everything is frozen, so make sure you provide them with water. An old, largish plant saucer makes an ideal container, for they will use it for bathing in as well as drinking. Break the ice on frosty mornings and top it up with warm, not hot, water so it will stay unfrozen for a while.

Don't feed birds between April and September. There is a lot of natural food around then, and the birds will have young, which can be harmed by some of the foods we may put out.

The carol concert/Christmas revue

Somehow, even if you hate singing, carol concerts are always great fun. It's all to do with the wonderful excitement of Christmas – apart from the summer holidays, the best time of the year.

If you can't sing or act, you can still become a Christmas revue star by making everyone laugh. Here's a selection of Christmas jokes with which to sleigh(!) your friends:

What was Father Christmas's wife called?
Mary Christmas.

What did one Christmas cracker say to its friend?
'My pop's bigger than your pop!'

What goes ho, ho, ho, bonk?
Father Christmas laughing his head off.

Why does Father Christmas come down the chimney?
Because it soots him.

What do you get if you cross Father Christmas with a cat?
Santa Claws!

What do you get if you cross a snowman with Jaws?
Frostbite!

How does Santa travel round the world?
By icicle.

What nationality is Santa Claus?
North Polish.

FRED: I got a wombat for Christmas.
TED: *What do you do with a wombat?*
FRED: Play wom, of course.

And, finally, did you hear about the tug of war team that only performed on 24 December? It was their Christmas 'eave!

All present and correct

Let's finish the autumn term with a few suggestions for Christmas presents for people you may find difficult to please. Remember that if you have time it is always better to make presents than to buy them, as people (especially older people) appreciate them so much more.

Almost everybody likes things to eat, such as chocolates and other sweets, nuts, little cakes, and so on, but don't give them to anyone who is on a diet! Almost everyone is happy with a book, too, but choose the right book for the right person. For example, you might give your younger brother a book of jokes, your mother a whodunnit (but check it isn't one she's got already), your dad a book of his favourite cartoons, or your grandparents a collection of old photographs. Here are some more specific ideas:

For a younger brother or sister
toys that make a noise
toys for the bath
toys that bounce
toys on wheels
building bricks
colouring books
picture books
glove puppets

For an older brother or sister
a pop poster
a record or cassette

TEACHER: Harriet, why is your homework in your mother's handwriting?

a book about their favourite pastime

a special magazine (e.g. a car magazine, or glossy
   fashion magazine)

bath salts/oils/soaps, etc.

bright socks/gloves

a scarf

cheap jewellery

For your best friend

something with their name or initial on, e.g. a T shirt or
   key-ring

a torch

an amusing pen or pencil

a notebook/address book/diary

something for a collection

a special book on their favourite subject (e.g. horses,
   pop stars, etc.)

a special calendar – ditto

For your Mum or Auntie

a small box of expensive chocolates

brightly-coloured pants

a potted plant

anything that smells nice, e.g. bath oil, talc, soap

china/glass or wooden ornaments

a pretty china plate

a jotter pad for her desk

For your Dad or Uncle

a mug

a book

large, brightly-coloured hankies

HARRIET: I borrowed her pen.

jazzy socks
a jotter pad for his desk
brightly-coloured paper clips
a labelling machine

For your grandparents
a magnifying glass
anything you've made yourself, e.g. a calendar, home-
    made sweets, etc.
speciality teas
prettily packed special biscuits
small pots of jam or honey
a picture frame for family photos

The Spring Term

TERM BEGINS ON .... ☹

DATES TO REMEMBER ....

Shrove Tuesday (pancake day) ....

14 February (St Valentine's Day) ....

Good Friday ....

Easter Day ....

All Fools' Day (1 April) ....

We break up for half term on ....

We go back after half term on ....

SPECIAL PROJECTS FOR THIS TERM ....

....

....

....

....

....

....

EXAM DATES THIS TERM ....

....

....

....

....

....

....

**FRIENDS' AND FAMILY BIRTHDAYS
THIS TERM** ....

....

....

....

....

....

....

....

....

....

TERM ENDS ON......................☺(FANTASTIC!)

People always feel a bit bleak at the beginning of the spring term. All the fun of Christmas is over, the food has been eaten, the presents enjoyed, and Easter looks an awfully long way ahead. But cheer up, there's lots of fun to be had this term, too. On Shrove Tuesday (in February or early March) you can make pancakes. You will find out how on page 65. There are also tips on surviving the school play, which is often staged this term, useful advice on coping with all your lovely Christmas loot, an amazing picture to complete, a special egg-cup to make for Easter, more classroom clangers, a hilarious selection of jokes, games to play at home or under the desk, and, of course, a good number of tips on basic survival during the hours between nine and four.

Netball

The tallest girls with the best aiming and throwing ability are usually those who are good at netball. If you're short and can't throw, you won't do very well, but the great thing about the game is that you can run up and down to keep warm, shadowing your opposite number (and holding a conversation with her if she happens to be your friend as well). You can also make a great deal of noise without doing anything constructive at all to score goals. The chances are that no one will either mind or notice.

Headmistress/headmaster

In the old days people summoned to the headmistress's or headmaster's study used to go prepared with a book shoved down their pants to protect them from the cane.

Fortunately caning doesn't happen in many schools today, but the headmistress/master is still a force to be reckoned with. Do your best not to antagonize her or him. Call them by their proper names or 'sir'. (Don't call women 'sir' or they'll think you're taking the mickey. Call them Miss Brown or Mrs Jones – especially if that is what their names are.) Above all, don't call them Old Fish Face, or whatever their nickname happens to be, or you may never come out of their study alive.

School magazine

Most of the articles in the school magazine will be written by people who like to add to their burden of work by writing long and dreary descriptions of this outing or that visit, missing out any of the amusing things that happened entirely. When I was at school we were once taken on a nature study ramble by a short, round teacher who got stuck in a stile – one of those constructed from two tall, upright stones with little space in between – and provided the class with the laugh of the year, but no mention of it ever made its way into the school magazine. Most school magazines print poems and examples of pupils' artistic efforts, too. If you are no poet, but really want to make your mark, try getting your cubist picture of Genghis Khan (really the maths master, but only fellow pupils know that) into the magazine. The whole school will fall about with laughter – only the teachers will be puzzled.

KATIE, VISITING THE ZOO: Shall I give the elephant one of the buns I made at school?

RI

RI stands for Religious Instruction, or what used to be called scripture. Its teaching varies a lot in different schools and in different parts of the country. Although the majority of people in England are nominally Christians, even if they don't go to church, in most schools there are people who are Jews, Muslims, and other religions. Whatever you think about religion, you should never make fun of anyone else's beliefs. Everyone has the right to carry out their acts of worship in their own way. Even if you have no religious upbringing of your own, you probably enjoy the music and language of the Church, and the Bible stories. After all, just about everyone likes Christmas carols and services, don't they?

Chemistry

Chemistry has lots of scope for fun and games. The only dreary thing about it is having to learn the symbols and formulae, though sometimes writing them on your hand will help. Knowing them can be useful, though, if only to avoid the fate of poor Billy Jones.

> Billy Jones is dead,
> We'll never see him more.
> For what he thought was H_2O*
> Was H_2SO_4.**

* water
** sulphuric acid – highly dangerous

KATIE'S FATHER: Why, what has it ever done to you?

If you play too many pranks in chemistry you may well suffer Billy's fate! If you are feeling particularly naughty, and are willing to risk punishment, you could try letting off a stink bomb in chemistry in order to confuse the teacher, who won't understand how such an awful smell can possibly be produced when you've only got as far as lighting the bunsen burners.

Managing your money

This is something we all have to learn how to do. Even governments have budgets! A budget simply means an estimate of your likely income and expenditure, and it can be done weekly, monthly or annually.

If you have read *David Copperfield* you may remember Mr Micawber's wise remark: 'Annual income £20, annual expenditure £19 19s. 6d., result, happiness. Annual income £20, annual expenditure £20 0s. 6d., result, misery.' Although our annual incomes are a bit more than £20 today, the sentiment expressed still holds good. If you can live within your income you can feel contented, if you get into debt, you will be miserable.

Budgeting is all about not getting into debt, by finding out what your income and expenditure are. Unless you earn money in your spare time (see page 94), your income will largely depend on your parents. You may get weekly or monthly pocket money from them, which may have to cover expenses like fares and school dinners, or may be simply for you to spend on luxuries such as sweets and comics. Start your budgeting by listing the money you get each week or month,

DARREN: It looks like rain.

including any you may earn, under the heading *Income*. Then, under the heading *Expenditure*, list all the things you spend money on in a week or a month. It is easier to start by considering a week and then multiplying it by four if you receive your pocket money monthly. Don't forget things like entrance fees to swimming baths, fares to go to Scouts or Guides, as well as expenses concerned with school and the buying of goodies.

Add up each column. If the income exceeds the expenditure you may feel that everything is all right, but if you have only budgeted for a week, stop for a moment and consider the longer term view. Next week there may be a birthday present to buy, at the end of the month an outing to save for, or you may know that before too long you will need new tyres on your bike. So it makes sense to try and save some of your money, so that when these things crop up you will be able to cope with them without too much hardship. If you think of budgeting in terms of a year, there will be Christmas to save up for, summer holidays to take into consideration, and possibly clothes or sports equipment to buy.

Saving money

You can save money in a piggy bank for day-to-day needs, but if you are saving up for something special over a long period of time, or if you have been given quite large sums of money for a birthday or Christmas, then it makes sense to open a savings account with a post office or a bank.

Savings accounts, or deposit accounts as they are called at banks, are a means of keeping your money

CAROL: Yes, but it says chicken soup on the packet.

safely and letting it earn interest. Interest rates vary, but a rate of 5% per annum means that £100 deposited in the bank for a year will earn £5 interest and therefore be worth £105 at the end of that year.

With a post office savings account you can choose either an 'ordinary' account or an 'investment' account. The latter pays a higher rate of interest but you have to give a month's notice if you want to draw the money out again.

Showers

Most school showers are pretty unpleasant. The room is usually cold, the water is not necessarily much hotter, and there's never anywhere dry to put your clothes. If you really can't bear the thought of a shower, take off your outer clothes, shoes and socks, wrap your towel round you over your underclothes, go into the shower, hang your towel over the curtain, turn on the water and keep well out of the way. You can usually angle the nozzle so it splashes down the cubicle wall instead of all over you. After a few minutes, wrap the towel back round yourself – you could damp it a bit for the sake of authenticity – turn the shower off and go back out again. If you do it carefully no one will ever know you haven't even got wet.

Punctuality

Teachers are very keen on punctuality, and some pupils are better at it than others. If you know you are going to be late, then it is as well to have some excuses up your sleeve (see *Excuses* page 106), but generally speaking it is better to be really late – say half an hour or more – than five or ten minutes, because your excuses then just might be true. You can push your luck with this as with everything, however, and if you are consistently half an hour late then your excuses will not be believed even on the day when the excuse is genuine – a bit like the tale of the boy who cried wolf.

If you are the kind of person who is always late and you genuinely want to change things, try setting your watch fifteen minutes fast and pretending it is correct. If you can't get up in the morning, buy a really loud alarm clock and *get up when it goes off* no matter how

60

strong the temptation to stay in bed. If your family get in the way then make your own breakfast and leave for school when *you* want to. Don't take any notice of the brother or sister who is trying to delay you, or ask your help with something, and don't be beguiled into watching breakfast television and then missing the bus.

Arithmetic

In a recent POP (Pupil Opinion Poll) arithmetic topped the list both as the most hated *and* most enjoyed subject. Impossible, you say? Well, of course, some pupils said one thing and some another. If you enjoy arithmetic and know you are good at it then you are a

PE TEACHER: Why didn't you stop the ball?

very lucky person, but if you are the type who can add up a column of figures three times and get three different answers, all you can do is try as hard as possible and just put up with it. Although we now have calculators and computers to help us, we still need a basic knowledge of arithmetic. The trouble with even the most sophisticated machinery is that it can go wrong, and also that it is at the mercy of the person using it, who may give it the wrong instructions. So it is still useful to be able to tell that if the machine says that $6 \times 100 = 60,000$ the answer is wrong. (If you can't see why the answer is wrong, I should give up all ideas of becoming a chartered accountant.)

Sewing/Needlework

If you are not very good at sewing then don't buy expensive materials – just in case you never get to wear the garments you are making. If you are clumsy, beware of pricking yourself on pins and needles and then getting blood all over the fabric – a red-spotted design in one corner will look very peculiar. Don't have races to see who can drive the electric sewing machine the fastest – this will not endear you to the teacher. Problems like sewing a waistband onto a gathered skirt and trying to keep the gathers even, or, worse, trying to set in a sleeve, are best taken very slowly and step-by-step – first pinning them in place, then tacking and finally machining or hand-sewing. If you do it in a hurry then you'll just make a mess of it and regret it.

Hand sewing and embroidery are meant to be neat. Don't go putting grubby hands all over the material

JIMMY: I thought that was what the goal net was for.

and sewing great loose floppy stitches and then wonder why it looks so awful. Wash your hands before you start and sew with small, even stitches. Fasten off the thread securely so the sewing doesn't all come undone again. If you have to sew on buttons, sew them securely too, or they may fall off and get lost as soon as you wear the garment.

One of the most difficult tasks is putting in a zip. The trick is to pin and tack it in place first, and then to sew along both sides of the zip from the closed end to the open end, rather than just sewing all the way round it in the same direction. This way, any tendency for the material to stretch enables it to stretch in the same direction along both sides, so you won't end up with the material along one side of the zip longer than that along the other.

Staff room

This is where the teachers congregate to say nasty things about the pupils over a cup of weak coffee and a cigarette. The idea of snooping round the staff room when they are not there is appealing, but the trouble is that some of them always seem to be there (they are probably shirking lessons, too) so it tends to be difficult. You could try ringing the fire bell and sneaking in after everyone has left the building if you are desperate to get in, but it's probably not worth risking the conse-quences.

SALLY: What makes you think your English teacher likes you?

Classroom clangers

Here's another collection of clangers from the work of pupils whose enthusiasm exceeded their accuracy. Let's start with some from the history exercise books:

The ancient Romans wore open-toed shoes called vandals.

Nelson commanded the Victory *and died. A plaque marks the spot at sea where he fell.*

Florence Nightingale was a nurse who used to sing in Berkeley Square.

The Vikings had horns on their heads and were known as Great Danes.

The Queen of England sat on a scone to be crowned.

Augustus remained in the same position for four years.

The Colossus of Rhodes is Spaghetti Junction.

The second wife of Henry VIII was Anne Berlin.

When he was getting old, Henry VIII had an abbess on each knee, which made it difficult for him to walk.

And here are some from the maths books:

Four points joined together make an equilateral triangle.

LXX stands for love and kisses.

A polygon is a dead parrot.

And some from the religious knowledge books:

The first commandment was when Eve told Adam to eat the apple.

Jacob's brother was called See-Saw.

A papal bull is a male cow owned by the Pope, who lives in the vacuum.

Faith is believing what you know to be untrue.

Noah's wife was Joan of Arc.

Insects is something that smells and is burnt in churches.

Pancake Day

Pancake Day is Shrove Tuesday, the day before the beginning of Lent, when Christians fast (or often give up a favourite food) for forty days to commemorate Christ's fast in the wilderness. Because of the fast people used to have a feast to use up their rich foods before it started, and that is how the tradition of making pancakes started.

Here's a basic recipe for pancakes. Why not invite your friends round for a pancake party? (Cooking with hot oil can be dangerous, so make sure an adult is always with you when you make pancakes. Remember, the kitchen is one place where you shouldn't fool around.)

PANCAKES
You Will Need
frying pan
palette knife
mixing bowl

fork
whisk (optional)
plates for serving

Ingredients (Makes 4)
100 g (4 oz) plain flour
1 egg
300 ml (½ pint) milk
1 tablespoon cooking oil
pinch salt
small amounts of oil for frying
castor sugar and lemon wedges for serving

Method
1. Sieve the flour into a mixing bowl and add the salt.
2. Make a hollow in the flour, crack the egg and drop it into the hollow.
3. Start adding the milk gradually and mix in the flour from the edges a little at a time with a fork.
4. When half the milk has been added, beat the mixture hard with a fork and add the oil. The mixture should be smooth, not lumpy.
5. Whisk in the rest of the milk, using either a whisk or a fork. Cover the bowl and leave it to stand in a cool place *for at least half an hour* before using.
6. Put a small amount of oil in a frying pan and heat it until it begins to smoke. Be very careful not to burn yourself.
7. Pour off any surplus oil so the bottom of the pan is barely covered, and, taking great care, wipe it out with a piece of kitchen roll.
8. Put the pan back on the heat, stir the batter and pour in just enough to give a thin pancake.
9. While it is cooking, loosen the edges with a palette knife. Flip the pancake over to cook the other side. It should be brown on both sides.

10. Slide the pancake onto a warmed plate, sprinkle it with castor sugar, and serve it with a wedge of lemon on the side of the plate to squeeze over it. The pancakes may also be stuffed with various fillings, or may be served with jam and cream.

Gym

Don't worry if you can't shin up a rope like a monkey, you'll find something you *can* do in the gymnasium, even if it is only climbing the wall bars. If you are lucky enough to have a trampoline in your school you can have a great time bouncing about, as long as you avoid putting your foot through the springs at the sides.

Vaulting over the horse or box, doing elegant hand-stands and somersaults on the rings and walking along a bar may be more than your muscles and balance can cope with. But most people can do a somersault on the ground, or hang from a bar by their hands and feet and 'walk' along it. The worst things about gym are the scratchy mats, the cold dank changing rooms and the smell of hot, dirty plimsolls!

Domestic science

In order to survive domestic science you need nerves of steel and a cast-iron stomach (see also *School dinners*, page 24). Warn your mother that it's no use thinking that whatever you are making in the lesson will do for supper and save her cooking, for it is most likely to be inedible, and on the rare occasions that something does

ENGLISH TEACHER: Now, Simon, can you spell your name backwards?

turn out to be good, it will be seized and wolfed down by the half-starved scavengers in your class. To help you survive this most traumatic of lessons, here are a few do's and don'ts.

Do
* Remember to take the ingredients of whatever you are making to school or you'll have to spend a boring lesson cleaning the saucepans.

SIMON: No, mis.

* Remember to put *all* the ingredients, in the right order, into whatever you are making. I once made a Swiss Roll without any flour in it. It rose up like a balloon in the oven and collapsed into a flat, shrivelled layer of nothingness when I took it out.
* Time whatever you are cooking. Otherwise the result may be another burnt offering.
* Check that the water doesn't boil dry when cooking vegetables or steamed puddings, etc. Otherwise you will have the same result, and a pan that will take you all day to clean. It's no use trying to hide it in a cupboard, teachers always discover them.

Don't

* Turn on a non-automatic gas oven at the main and then wander off to find something to light it with, stopping for a chat on the way. If you do, you'll blow up the classroom (and yourself, if you like the idea of blowing up the classroom).
* Put rat poison in the demonstration cake the teacher is taking home to eat, *however much you may be tempted.*
* Put a tin of cheap cat food in the shepherd's pie you are baking for the staff lunch (*h.m.y.m.b.t.*).
* Swap the food you have cooked badly (i.e. it's either burnt to a cinder or not cooked at all) for your enemy's golden brown and appetising dish (*h.m.y.m.b.t.*). Retribution might be swift and terrible.
* Drop the potatoes on the floor, scoop them up and mash them, saying the black bits of grit are black pepper (not if someone is going to have to eat them, anyway).

TEACHER: What does the word 'allocate' mean, Thomas?

Pencil and paper games

These can be essential for survival in times of desperate boredom. Here are some games that are fun to play, and reasonably unobtrusive if you are tempted to play them under the desk.

Noughts and crosses
Everyone knows how to play noughts and crosses, but have you ever tried giant noughts and crosses? You can use as many squares as there is room for on your paper.

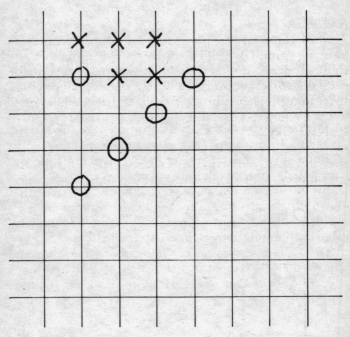

THOMAS: It's what you say when you meet someone called Catherine.

70

Simply draw lines across and down the paper to start with to make a large grid. When you play, you write your nought or cross on the point where two lines cross (see example, below), and the object is to get five 0s or five Xs in a straight line, either vertically, horizontally or diagonally. Cross off each row as you complete it, otherwise the game will get terribly confusing! As the paper begins to fill up it becomes increasingly difficult to prevent your opponent getting five in a line while you are planning your strategy. A good game for a long and boring lesson or assembly.

Hangman

A word game for two players based on the practice of hanging criminals from a gibbet (see diagram). You think of a word, and write it down as a row of dots, with each dot corresponding to a letter. Your opponent has to try and guess the word by finding out its components, letter by letter. For example, if your word is COMPANION, you write . . . . If your opponent says 'A', you write a letter A above the fifth dot. If he or she says 'O', you write an O above the second and eighth dots. If he or she says 'B', you draw in the first

part of the gibbet. Each part of the gibbet, and of the man, count for each wrong letter guessed (on the drawing there are eleven chances) and the object is to guess all the letters before you are hanged.

Boxes

This game is best played by two people, though three or four can play. To start with, create a large square out of dots on a piece of paper by drawing eleven dots, spaced approximately one centimetre apart, along the top of the paper. Draw ten more rows under this top row. If all the dots were joined up into squares you would now have 100 small squares.

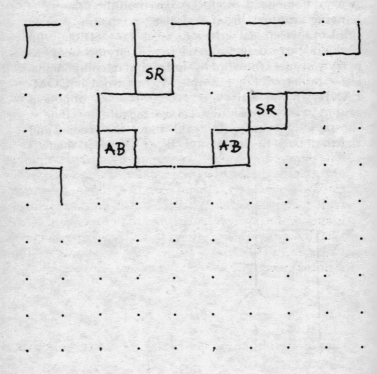

Each player takes a turn to join two dots with a line, the object being to complete a box. However, it is necessary to avoid being the player who draws the third line on a box, because then it falls to the opponent. When a player has completed a box, then he or she initials it, and has an extra go. If this extra turn completes another box they have a further turn. As the dotted square fills with boxes the game gets more and more exciting. The winner is the player who completes the greatest number of boxes.

Consequences

This game is great fun to play at a party, with a number of people, or it can be played just with two. Each player needs a piece of paper and a pen or pencil.

At the top of the paper each player writes a man's/boy's name. It could be someone famous or someone they know. They then fold over the top of the paper, so the name is hidden, and write 'met'. The paper is then passed on to the next player. If several people play, then the papers should be passed round in a circle. A woman's or girl's name is now added to the paper, folded over to hide it, and the word 'at' written below. The papers are passed round again. This time the name of a place is added, the paper folded and the words 'he said' written down. Then a remark is added, the paper folded, and 'she said' is written down. Another remark is added, the paper is folded, and 'and the consequence was' is written down. The players then enter the final happening, which can be as silly as you like. The eventual result might read something like this:

FRENCH TEACHER: What does *moi aussi* mean, William?

Bob Geldof

MET

Mrs Briggs (the maths teacher)

at

SAINSBURYS

He said

"I'd like a cucumber sandwich"

SHE SAID

"There's a funny smell in here"

and the consequence was

THEY BOTH SET TO WORK TO DIG
THE CHANNEL TUNNEL

Writing

Writing really means two things: the physical task of producing words on paper, and the mental task of creating in your brain what your hand is going to write on the paper. (If you've just been playing Consequences you'll know what I mean!)

The physical task of writing used to be governed by a lot of rules. Letters were supposed to be formed in certain ways, the writing was supposed to be either vertically upright or sloping slightly to the right (sloping back to the left was a cardinal sin), and pupils used to write with dip-in pens to which a new nib could be fitted when the old one got unbearably scratchy. These pens were dipped into ink-wells which sat in a hole on the right-hand side of the desk (too bad if you were left-handed) and a pupil appointed as ink monitor would refill the ink-wells from time to time. Bored pupils would sometimes amuse themselves with soaking little bits of blotting paper in the ink-well and flicking it across the room with a ruler. Although many of the old rules and practices no longer apply, it is still important for writing to be reasonably neat and easy to read, for if no one can read what you have written there is not much point in having written it, is there?

The creative task of writing takes thought, imagination and a quiet time in which to think about what you want to say. Some people find it very difficult. If you are one of them, the best tip is to think about the subject on which you are supposed to be writing and jot down anything at all that comes to mind connected with it. From these notes you should be able to build up some kind of picture, and be able to form a framework around which to write. (See *Essays*, page 97.)

Why did the boys dislike their PE teacher?

Swimming

There's one way to survive swimming, and that is don't stay under the water for too long! Most people enjoy swimming, but some people are braver about it than others. If you are one of the brave ones, never bully anyone who's afraid, and don't lark about pushing them under or playing tricks on them, pretending, for example, to help them float and then letting them go. Nothing is more terrifying to someone who is nervous in the water. And never, ever, push anyone into a swimming pool unless you know for certain that they are a good, strong swimmer.

Practise your swimming and try to gain your life-saving certificates. But never take risks in the water. Don't show off and try to show your friends how clever you are. If you swim in the sea, then only do so where you know it is safe. Some areas mark beaches that are dangerous for swimming, so never be tempted to try them out. Other areas, such as parts of Cornwall, are subject to freak currents, so again, take special care.

Because he thought the answer to everything was, 'gym'll fix it'.

76

Make sure an adult knows what you are doing if you are going swimming in the sea. Never swim straight out to sea, never swim when the tide is going out, and never go out with an inflatable airbed. *At all times in the water it is better to be safe than sorry.*

THIS TERM'S PROJECT

An Easter chicken egg-cup

You will need:
3 pieces of stiff white or brown paper 12 cm × 6 cm
a tube from the inside of a toilet roll or kitchen roll
Pritt Multi-Glue
Pritt Stick
pencil
ruler
scissors
red, yellow and black crayons, felt-tip pens or paints, or small pieces of red and yellow paper in place of them

1. Carefully cut a 3-cm length from the end of the tube. Discard the rest.
2. Using Pritt Multi-Glue, stick two of the pieces of paper together by gluing a 2-cm wide strip down each of the 6-cm sides and putting a few dabs of glue along *one* of the long sides.
3. Lightly mark the central 4 cm along the *unglued* edge, measure 3 cm above it and mark another central 4 cm, so you now have the corners of a square (see the diagram, above). This part will wrap round the cardboard tube.

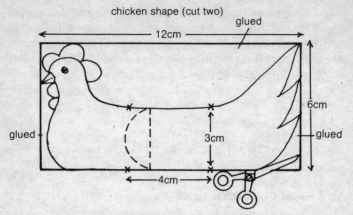

chicken shape (cut two)

glued

12cm

glued

glued

6cm

3cm

4cm

Dotted line shows fixing for front edge of wings

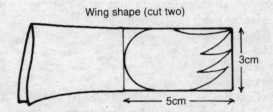

Wing shape (cut two)

3cm

5cm

4. Draw the outline of a chicken shape on either side of the central square, giving her a rather long body. Outline the eye, wattles (the loose red skin on the chicken's head and neck), beak and tail feathers as shown.

5. Holding these two pieces of paper carefully so they don't slip, cut out the chicken shape. Copy the markings onto the other side so the two sides match.

6. Fold the remaining piece of paper in two. Mark out a rectangle 5 cm long by 3 cm deep, and draw the wing shape on it. Cut it out carefully, including the feather edge.

7. Colour in the chicken's wattles red, its beak yellow and its eye black with crayons, felt-tip pens or paints. Alternatively you can trace, then cut out the wattle shapes in red paper and a beak shape in yellow paper, and glue them in place with Pritt Stick.

8. Now spread Pritt Multi-Glue on the outside of the roll and fit it into the central part of the chicken's body. Then carefully glue together the parts of the body, head and tail that are not yet stuck.

9. Glue along the inner curve of each wing using Pritt Multi-Glue and stick the one wing on each side of the body as shown in the diagram.

10. Your egg-cup is now all ready for Easter! If you have enough time you could make one for each member of the family and cook them boiled eggs on Easter morning.

The finished chicken egg-cup

TEACHER: How many seasons are there in a year?

The school play

If you're chosen to play a part in the play, and don't want to, then you can usually get the drama teacher to change his or her mind by being incapable of re-membering a single line, by mysteriously disappearing at rehearsal times, or by getting constant 'sore throats', so that only a croak comes out as you try to speak someone's immortal lines. (This takes a bit of practice but you'll manage it if you're determined enough.) If, on the other hand, you are not chosen and would like to have been, you may be able to get someone else in the play to put in a word for you, stressing your acting ability, though if the teacher knows you can never remember your tables or a single line of poetry by heart, never mind which day of the week it is, this is not likely to be effective.

If you are in the play, then don't try and confuse other people in it by coming out with lines from last year's production. Don't get greasepaint over the costumes or deliberately go on stage with the wrong make-up, e.g. an old man if you are meant to be the young hero, or vice versa. Don't pretend you can see without your specs if you can't. You might end up delivering an impassioned speech to a piece of scenery while your opposite number stands open-mouthed further off. Note the whereabouts of anything you may fall over, whether you're short-sighted or not, or you may get more laughs than you bargained for. Don't eat a hot curry or anything else full of onions and garlic if you don't want your fellow Thespians to recoil in horror as you breathe over them.

If you want to be really evil, on the other hand, you could try tacking the costumes together with loose thread so no one can get into them, fastening any doors on stage so no one can walk through them, or interfering with the flats so they fall down when touched.

April Fool!

To bring the spring term to a hilarious close, here are three April Fool jokes to play on your friends. Remember to play them before 12 o'clock, though, or the joke is on you!

Help! A spider!

This is a very simple joke requiring neither preparation nor equipment. All you do is point towards the corner of the room and shriek: 'Aaaaaaarrrrrggggghhhh! Look at that *huge* spider! Help!' Leap up onto a chair or your desk, if you're in class, and everyone else will follow suit. Let them get carried away for a minute or two, then shout: 'April Fool!'

Funny number

Try this one on a friend who is proud of his or her mathematical prowess, but only if they're not as good as they think they are. If anyone is really good at maths they may see through it!

Give your friend a piece of paper and a pencil, and say you are going to ask them to perform a simple task. All they have to do is to write on the paper, the number

MRS SMITH: What's your son going to be when he's passed all his exams?

81

eleven thousand, eleven hundred and eleven. Most people will write 11,1111. Is this right?

No, of course it isn't! The correct way to write it is 12,111. April Fool to you and your friend!

Severed finger

This is a really gruesome trick that you should only try out on people with strong stomachs. The idea is to persuade them that you are carrying round in your pocket a matchbox containing a severed finger! Ugh!

You will need an ordinary small matchbox, some cotton wool, a pair of scissors, and a red felt-tip pen. Empty the matches out of the box and put them in a safe place. At one end of the underneath of the inner drawer of the matchbox cut a hole large enough to poke a finger through – either your index finger or your middle finger would be suitable. Then, on the underside of the matchbox's cover, cut a U-shaped slot. Put the matchbox back together again, remembering to keep the hole and the slot underneath.

With the felt-tip pen, make some red marks on the cotton wool, to look like blood. Then draw a jagged line round the finger you are going to pretend is severed. Put the cotton wool in the matchbox, poke your finger through the hole, and you are ready to play the trick. Before you start, make sure the cover is on the matchbox.

Keep the hand with the matchbox on it in your pocket until you meet someone on whom to play the trick. Then tell them the story about the severed finger, and carefully bring the matchbox out of your pocket so your friend cannot tell your finger is in it. Open the box

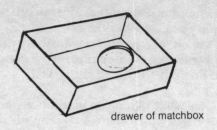

drawer of matchbox

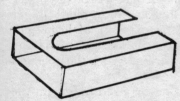

cover upside-down showing slot

cover right way up showing slot

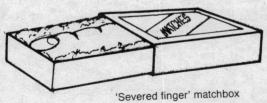

'Severed finger' matchbox

with your other hand, to reveal the finger in all its gory glory! You could even say that the finger is still alive, even though it's been severed, and wiggle it to prove the fact. When your friend goes pale, whip off the matchbox and say, 'April Fool!' before he or she faints!

Join the dots to see what's going on in this classroom on 1 April!

The Summer Term

TERM BEGINS ON .... ☹

DATES TO REMEMBER ....

1 May (Bank Holiday) ....

Spring Bank Holiday ....

We break up for half-term on ....

We go back after half term on ....

Our sports day is on ....

Our open day is on ....

Our prize-giving is on ....

SPECIAL PROJECTS FOR THIS TERM ....

....

....

....

....

....

....

EXAM DATES FOR THIS TERM ....

....

....

....

....

....

....

FRIENDS' AND FAMILY BIRTHDAYS
THIS TERM ....

....

....

....

....

....

....

....

....

....

....

TERM ENDS ON... ☺

(BEST DAY OF THE YEAR!)

Unless you are working for important exams, the summer term is the best of the year. There are lots of outdoor activities, sports day, and the wonderful, long summer holiday to look forward to. Because it is such an outdoor time, this term's project is how to make a kite, and there are tips on overhauling your bike and riding it safely, as well as some useful ideas on how to earn money for your holidays. There are also more classroom clangers, a feast of jokes, and, of course, lots of useful tips about school.

French

Unless you have an awful teacher, French can be great fun. For a start, it will enable you to crack jokes like this one:

> Frappe, frappe.
> *Qui est là?*
> Lors.
> *Lors qui?*
> Yes, that's why I can't open the door!

Formidable, n'est-ce pas? Don't worry about trying to learn French. Never mind if you can't make the 'eu' sound with the tendons in your throat all standing out, just wait until you get your French student teacher. These poor souls are not many years older than you are, and have to stand in front of the whole class trying to converse with the pupils in French. They are strangers to your school and to your country, and you will find that you can tease them unmercifully. The situation is made even worse (from their point of view) or better (from yours) if they are of the opposite sex to the pupils, because then you can really have a *jour de champs* (field day, what else?). Try saying, *'Vous êtes très jolie, mademoiselle'*, or *'Comme vous êtes beau, monsieur'*, and watch

90

them blush as, covered in confusion, they try and tell you off. Of course, you won't understand them when they do try and tell you off, so you are safe unless you push your luck and they bring the French teacher in on their side. If this happens you just have to grit your teeth and take your punishment, even if it's learning six irregular verbs by heart before the next French lesson.

Bells

Whether it's a bell on the top of a tower, a brass handbell or merely an electronic buzzer, most schools have a bell of some sort to summon you to lessons and to announce the end of them (yippee!). Intrepid pupils can occasionally cause chaos and confusion by hiding handbells, or wrapping padding round their clappers so they don't sound. Electronic bells can sometimes be silenced by inserting pieces of cardboard between the hammer and the bell, but to do this you really need to be a bit of an electrician. As for the bells on school towers, these are best left alone unless you are an expert rock climber.

Beware of . . .

The following are just a few of the things you need to be on your guard against while at school:

Teachers with steely-blue eyes
Over-friendly teachers
Over-unfriendly teachers

HISTORY TEACHER: Why were the Dark Ages so called?

Almost any other kind of teacher
School caretakers (usually grumpy old men)
Strange men, whether grumpy and old or young and good-looking, who hang around outside the school gates

JEMIMA: Because there were so many knights, Miss.

Friends who want to borrow money
Friends who want to borrow other things and then lose them
People who tell tales

Algebra

Algebra is much more fun than arithmetic. You can get quite fond of all those xs, as and bs that seem to live such extraordinary lives. *Why* is x such a mysterious character that no one knows what it is, and has to go through such extraordinary contortions to find out? Seriously, though, and perhaps surprisingly, algebra does have some relevance to life after school, so it is worth learning the basic principles even if it seems slightly ridiculous to you now.

Black and blue

Try this trick on a friend.
YOU: I bet I can make you say the word BLACK.
FRIEND: *I bet you can't.*
YOU: I bet you £10 I can.
FRIEND: *OK, try.*
YOU: What are the colours of the Union Jack?
FRIEND: *Red, white and blue.*
YOU: See! I told you I'd make you say BLUE.
FRIEND: *No you didn't. You said you'd make me say BLACK. Oops!*
YOU: I think I've won the bet!

FATHER: Clarence, do you need help with your homework?

Earning money

If you feel you would like more pocket money, or you want to save up for something special, then it is a good idea to earn some for yourself. But before you rush out to try and find a job, bear in mind that there are laws governing the employment of young people. Except in certain special cases, such as working on your parents' farm or agricultural holding, you have to be 13 years old before you can be employed. And even then you cannot work before 7 am or after 7 pm, or for more than two hours on a school day or a Sunday.

Some children think it's a good idea to ask their parents for money for helping with tasks around the house and garden, but this seems a bit unfair when you think of all your parents do for you. If you want to do this kind of work then it is better to ask people around your neighbourhood. Your parents might help by approaching some of the neighbours on your behalf, or you could be very enterprising and carefully write out little 'handbills' advertising your services, which you could slip through local letterboxes. Don't forget to put your name, address and phone number on it, though, or your potential clients will not be able to contact you. Your advertisement might look something like the one on the next page.

CLARENCE: No thanks, I'd rather get it wrong on my own.

```
            CARS  CLEANED

            GARDENS  WEEDED

            LAWNS  CUT

            DOGS  WALKED

            ERRANDS  RUN

by 14-year-old saving up for a new bike!
```

Contact

```
John Hames, 22 Alderney Crescent

Tel. 29681

out of school hours
```

Here are some other jobs you might be able to do to earn some money:

Paper round
Milk round on Saturdays
Working in a local shop/supermarket after school and on Saturdays
Cleaning houses
Sweeping up, etc. in the local hairdresser's on Saturdays
Working at the local riding school (this is usually in exchange for rides, not money)
Baby sitting
Fruit picking (summer/autumn only!)
Looking after pets while people are on holiday
Helping with decorating
Helping with children's parties

Tennis

Tennis is played by two or four players, on either grass or a hard court, and it is derived from a fourteenth-century game now called 'real tennis', which used to be played in England and France. The fact that modern tennis is more real to most people than real tennis just adds to the confusion, but it is when it comes to scoring that things get really difficult. For a player cannot score nil, he or she scores 'love'. It is believed that this word comes from the French for 'egg', *l'oeuf*, which is what O looks like, but this may not be true.

The first point scored in tennis is not 1 but 15; the second is 30, and the third not 45, as you might imagine, but 40. If, after that, the winning player scores the next point then he or she has won that game. If the losing player scores it then the score is deuce (the deuce it is!) and one of the players has to score two more consecutive points in order to win the game.

Tennis matches are divided into sets, with one player having to win six games, and at least two games more than the other player, before a set is won. A match consists of the best of three sets in women's tennis, and the best of five in men's. It is one of the few modern sports that differentiates between men and women.

If you don't like tennis, lobbing the ball high up into the air over into the next court but one, or, if you are playing in a public park, into the boating lake, should ensure that you spend the rest of the game searching for it. If you make a habit of this you may even be banned from playing altogether.

Those who think they are good at tennis often show off and try and play like Wimbledon stars, grunting and groaning as they hit the ball, tapping their racquets on their shoes, etc. They'll also try to leap over the net after they've won, to shake hands with the loser. But wait a moment. If the net just happens to be a bit higher than they thought it was, they will catch a toe in it and go sprawling on the ground on the far side. This is particularly effective on hard courts.

Write ear!

Try this trick on a friend. Brandish a pencil and a piece of paper and say to them, 'I can write with my right ear!' The friend will not believe you, and will probably challenge you to prove it. All you do is pick up the pencil and paper and write on it:

With my right ear

Simple, isn't it?

Essays

Teachers often set very uninspiring subjects for essays, like 'what I did in the school holidays'. You sit and think about it, and unless something unusual happened, or you went somewhere exciting on holiday, you can't think of a single thing to write about at all. After all, an essay that said, 'I played football, went swimming and helped Dad in the garden' doesn't sound too exciting, does it? But stop and think about it for a few moments, and list everything you can remember that happened. Perhaps during one of your football games you had to go and fetch the ball from someone's garden

ENGLISH TEACHER: Kate, make up a sentence using the word 'lettuce'.

97

and met a strange old man whom you thought might be a spy. Perhaps when you were swimming you managed five lengths for the first time, and felt terribly pleased and proud. Perhaps with your gardening you managed to grow vegetables which tasted delicious – you may even have cooked them yourself and impressed the whole family. If you put details like this into your essay it will make fascinating reading.

Having got your list, plan a basic structure for the essay. You need to work out a beginning, a middle and an end, and to rough out what each part will include. After that all you have to do is to sit down and write it!

But supposing nothing exciting at all happened to you? Well, you are supposed to be producing a piece of creative writing, so you can always exaggerate slightly or invent a few amazing incidents. Who knows, you may end up becoming a famous novelist!

Free periods

Some schools actually allow pupils to have free periods, though not usually until you are in the senior school. If you are lucky enough to be at such a school, then make the most of your free periods. You can read your favourite books, write letters, compile your Christmas lists, do your homework(!), draw pictures, plot campaigns against the maths teacher, or play consequences or other games, though in most schools you will not get away with running a poker school.

Of course, what you are supposed to be doing is studying, doing extra work on those subjects you are

KATE: Please lettuce out of school early today, Miss.

weak in, so if you are supervised, it is as well to hide your copy of *Beano* inside your history book.

On your bike

If you do not ride your bike much in winter, then give it a thorough overhaul before you set out on long summer trips. The following are the things you should check regularly:

1. Examine the brakes and make sure they are set correctly.
2. Check the tyres for stones and cuts, and check the pressure. On most bikes it should be around 40 lb per sq in.
3. Check that the lights are working.
4. Make sure the handlebars are positioned correctly.
5. Make sure the saddle is adjusted to the right height.
6. Oil the working parts with special oil sold for cycles. The bicycle should be lubricated at the following points: the small hole on the front-wheel hub, which is covered with a spring clip; the pivot point on the front and back brakes, keeping oil off the brake blocks or rims; the bearings on which the front forks turn in the head tube (check that there isn't too much play in them); between the brake cables and outer covers; the bottom bracket bearings; the pedals; and the freewheel unit. If your bicycle has no oiling points on its hubs, pedals or bottom bracket it is because it has sealed bearings which should not need attention, though check there is no play in them.

TEACHER: Percy, you must learn to give and take.

Cycling road safety

1. If you are going to ride on a road, make sure you know the Highway Code. It applies to you as well as to car drivers.

2. Make sure your bike is in good working order (see previous section). Fit it with a bell to warn people of your approach.

3. Before you pull away from the kerb, move out into the road, or turn right or left, always glance behind you to check that it is safe to do so. Give clear arm signals of your intentions.

4. If you are riding at night, wear reflective clothing, including arm bands so your signals can be seen.

5. Ride in single file on busy, narrow roads, and never more than two abreast on wider roads.

6. Unless you are signalling, keep both hands on the handlebars. Always keep both feet on the pedals.

7. Don't ride close behind another vehicle.

8. Don't hold on to another vehicle or another cyclist.

9. Don't lead an animal from your bike. It is cruel to the animal, and dangerous too.

10. Don't carry anything which may upset your balance or become entangled in the wheels or chain.

PERCY: I did. I gave him a black eye and took his bar of chocolate.

History

As just about everybody knows, Henry Ford said that history was bunk. Someone else who summed it up rather neatly was Ambrose Bierce, compiler of the *Devil's Dictionary*, who defined it as 'An account mostly false, of events mostly unimportant, which are brought about by rulers mostly knaves, and soldiers mostly fools.'

Your history teacher, of course, would not publicly agree with these definitions, though he or she might secretly agree with parts of them. The great thing about history is the fascinating look it gives us into other people's lives, and the remarkable thing about it is that it shows us that even thousands of years ago people had a lot in common with us today. The main trouble with history is learning all the dates when things happened.

For some reason everyone in England can remember the date 1066, and some can even remember 1815 (the

Battle of Trafalgar, dumbo). But why can't we remember when James I reigned, or when the Corn Laws were repealed? One way is to write the dates on your hands before lessons or exams, in code if need be. Then if you are noticed looking at the palm of your hand and the teacher only sees a lot of meaningless squiggles he or she will not know that they are really the dates of the French Revolution. As for which king of England came after which, you could try this rhyme:

> Willy, Willy, Harry, Stee,
> Harry, Dick, John, Harry Three;
> One, Two, Three Neds, Richard Two,
> Henry Four, Five, Six, then who?
> Neds Four, Five and Dick the Bad,
> Harrys Twain and Ned the Lad.
> Mary, Bessie, James the Vain,
> Charley, Charley, James Again.
> William and Mary, Anna Gloria,
> Four Georges, William, and Victoria.
> Edward Seventh – and then –
> George the Fifth in 1910!

After which you only have to remember Edward VIII, the king who never was, George VI, and Elizabeth II, which isn't too difficult, is it?

Classroom clangers

A final collection of hilarious howlers from the unreliable pens of those poor misguided schoolboys and girls. To begin with, some gaffs from the science books:

Mercury was an ancient Greek god who can now be found inside a thermometer.

102

A cuckoo lays other birds' eggs in its nest.

Magnesia is a disease when you can't remember anything.

Blood is made up of red and white corkscrews.

Tadpoles eat one another until they become frogs.

Newton discovered gravity when an apple fell out of a tree and struck him as being curious.

Atom bombs are made from geraniums.

Moths eat hardly nothing, except holes.

The pancreas is an infernal organ.

And here are some more from the English books:

Homer wrote a famous play called the Oddity. He was Greek, but Livid was a Roman poet.

People who live in Paris are called Parisites.

An allegory is when you get a rash after eating things like strawberries.

Well-behaved children should never crumble their bread or roll in their soup.

A conservative is a glass porch on a house.

My uncle lived to be a centurion.

My father communicates to work in London every day on the train.

The Stock Market is where cattle, sheep and pigs are bought and sold.

JIMMY: I've thought of a way of improving our cricket team.

A dog will not bite your hand or wag its tail unless it likes you.

An allegation is when a lot of alligators lie in wait for you.

And finally, a wonderful collection from the history books:

The Spanish Mane was another name for the King of Spain's beard, which was singed by Sir Francis Drake.

Mary I's nickname was Broody Mary.

In England wine was drunk by noblemen, but in France even the pheasants drank it.

GAMES MASTER: Oh good. Are you leaving?

Karl Marx was the Marx brother who played the harp.

Beau Brummel was a well-dressed man from Birmingham.

In 1675 Frederick William defeated a Swedish army twice his size.

If Queen Victoria were alive she'd turn over in her grave.

School medicals

Everybody dreads these, but there's no way to avoid them, you just have to grit your teeth and bear them (and usually yourself as well). You may have reached an age when you will not allow even your parents to see you without clothes on, never mind a school doctor, but you just have to realize that the school doctors see hundreds of bodies just like yours every week and find nothing extraordinary about it at all. So grin and bare your all, and be thankful when it's over. There's no point in trying to cheat in the eye test, either, because even if someone tells you what the chart says, they will probably change the chart just before you go in. They will then think there's something very peculiar about your eyes if you read A for M, E for O, and so on. Or they'll just tell you off for cheating. So don your clean underwear and be brave.

What's the definition of a mushroom?

Excuses

We all need these at times. Here is a collection of some of the best – but don't blame me if they don't work!

For being late

The alarm didn't go off.

The clock radio has fused.

Dad woke me up when he went out at six, but I fell asleep again until nine.

The buses are on strike.

The train was cancelled.

I forgot my homework and had to go back for it.

I wasn't feeling well and had to spend a long time in the lavatory.

My mother's ill and I had to wait until the doctor had been so that I could take her prescription to the chemist.

We forgot to put the clocks forward.*

For non-delivery of homework

I left it on the bus/at home.

I posted it by mistake instead of the letters.

The dog ate it.

My friend was at our house last night and must have taken it with her, I couldn't find it after she'd gone.

I had a Chinese take-away for supper and was ill all evening.

I left my pen at school and couldn't find another in the whole house.

* Only use this at the appropriate time.

A school dining-hall.

We had a burst pipe and I had to help Dad keep a plug in the hole until the plumber came and then I was told to go to bed.

The cat was sick on it.

For talking in class

I was just asking her what you'd said, as I didn't hear you properly.

I wasn't talking, I was answering.

I wasn't talking, just practising my ventriloquism technique.

He/she only asked the time, Miss.

For bad behaviour at school

He/she said if I didn't do it I'd be sorry.

Everyone else was doing it too.

I was sitting there reading my set book when the two of them bumped into me.

My desk just collapsed, of course I didn't saw the legs in half.

I was bending down to pick my pencil off the floor – I didn't know those comic postcards were there. I've never seen them before.

I had a box of matches in case there was a power cut. I didn't mean to burn the classroom down, honest.

(*If caught eating in class*) I shan't have time for lunch as we have to rehearse the school play.

I thought that was the cleaner's bucket of water. I expect someone put it on top of the door in case someone fell over it.

He hit me first, it was self-defence.

My hat blew off because it was windy.

I had to run down the corridor to get to the loo in time.

I didn't call Miss X by a rude name, I said I had an itch.

For not doing as your parents want you to do

Teacher said we must all watch this programme.

In our domestic science class we were told that this kind of food is bad for you.

I was reading in bed because I couldn't sleep for worrying about the exams – it was one of my set books.

I can't wash up, I have to be at a rehearsal of the school play.

I've been working so hard at school I need to sleep late at the weekends.

I was concentrating so hard on my homework I didn't realize the potatoes had boiled over.

I have to play the record player loud when I'm doing my homework to drown the noise of the television.

I can't come with you to Uncle Tony's/carry the shopping/help with the chores because I have so much school work to do.

Use this page to draw a picture of your ideal school. It can be as fanciful as you like. For example, if you think each classroom should have a fizzy drinks dispenser, draw one in. Or, if you think the school should be surrounded by a moat in which to throw unwanted teachers, draw that in too.

THIS TERM'S PROJECT

A kite to fly

You will need
1.75 metres of 0.6 cm square-section dowelling
1 metre of 90-cm wide crêpe paper or lightweight cloth
40 metres lightweight nylon line
small lightweight ring
ruler
measuring tape
pencil
Pritt Multi-Glue
Scissors

1. Mark the dowelling into one length of 90 cm and one length of 84 cm (there should be just 1 cm left over) and get an adult to saw off the lengths for you. Then ask them to cut a small notch in each end of both pieces.
2. Measure and mark the centre of the 84-cm spar, and measure and mark 15 cm from one end of the 90-cm spar. With a short length of the nylon line tie the two spars together at this point, wrapping the line round firmly.
3. Now take another piece of line and tie it round the outer edges of the spars, passing it through the notches to make a framework. Fasten the line securely.
4. Lie the framework on the paper or fabric and carefully draw a line round the shape. With the scissors, cut out the shape, leaving about 2 cm to allow for the paper or fabric to be wrapped round the framework. At each corner cut a small V shape into the paper or fabric as far as the line you have drawn.

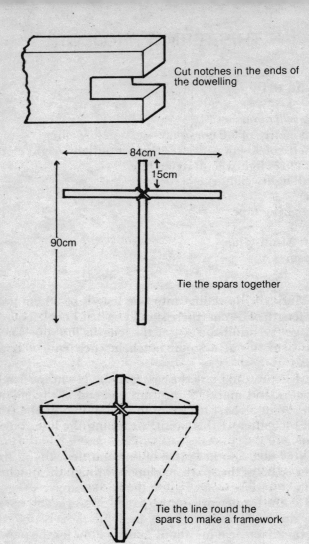

Cut notches in the ends of the dowelling

84cm

15cm

90cm

Tie the spars together

Tie the line round the spars to make a framework

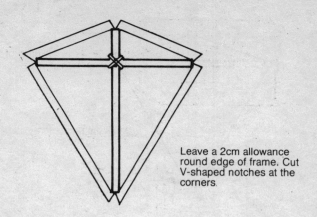

Leave a 2cm allowance
round edge of frame. Cut
V-shaped notches at the
corners.

5. Spread Pritt Multi-Glue over the edge of the paper
or fabric as far as the line you have drawn. Lie the
framework on the paper or fabric and carefully fold the
glued part over and press down, to attach the cover to
the framework.

6. On the outer side of the fabric cover, mark where the
spars cross, and make another mark 5 cm up from the
bottom of the kite. Make small holes through the cover
at these points. Cut a 40-cm length of line, pass it
through the cover, and attach one end of it to the point
where the spars cross. Cut a 70-cm length, pass it
through the lower hole, and tie it to the spar. Attach the
free ends of both these lines to the ring.

7. Now tie a piece of line across the back of the kite from

TEACHER: What is the meaning of coup de grâce?

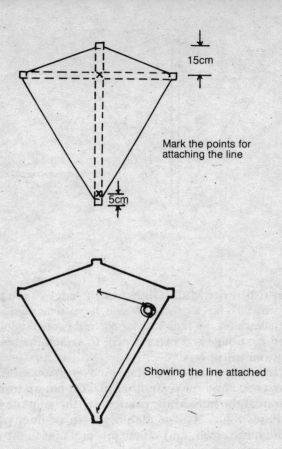

15cm

Mark the points for
attaching the line

5cm

Showing the line attached

one end of the horizontal spar to the other, pulling it
tight enough to bow the kite. Fasten it securely.
8. All that remains is to tie the end of the line to the ring
– and there is your kite ready to fly.

SHEILA: It's French for lawnmower, Miss.

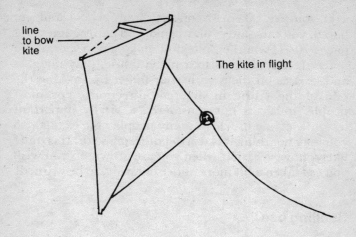

line
to bow
kite

The kite in flight

Music

If you can't stand music lessons then you could try
suggesting a lesson on the relevance of classical music
to modern music and spend the time listening to pop
records. However, your teacher will probably see
through this ploy. Actually, if you try listening properly
to classical music you may discover that a lot of it is
very enjoyable, and wonder why you thought you
didn't like it.

The worst part of music lessons is singing aloud in
front of the rest of the class, and the worst part of *this* is
sight-reading aloud. Short of having permanent laryn-
gitis it is difficult to see how you can avoid it per-
manently, but you could try complaining of a bad
throat for one lesson and after that making such a
horrendous noise when you sing that it is painful for
your listeners. That will probably stop them from
asking you too often.

If you are taken to concerts from school and get bored, you can always play pencil and paper games (see pages 70–74) on the pretext of making notes, or, if the seats are upholstered in a plush fabric, play noughts and crosses on them with your finger by stroking the pile of the fabric in different directions. For most people, music is not considered a vitally important lesson (i.e. one in which many people take exams), so you may not think it is worth bothering with. It is quite likely, however, that when you are grown up you wish you *had* taken a bit more notice of music, so be warned!

Spelling bee

How good is your spelling and that of your friends? Test it by trying out the following trick:

YOU: How do you spell the word 'joke'?
FRIEND: *J, O, K, E.*
YOU: How do you spell the word 'poke'?
FRIEND: *P, O, K, E.*
YOU: How do you spell the word 'folk'?
FRIEND: *F, O, L, K.*
YOU: How do you spell the white of an egg?
FRIEND: *Y, O, L, K.*
YOU: But that's the yellow part of an egg!

The Country Code

On summer weekends, and in the holidays, you may go on trips to the countryside, to picnic, walk or just explore. If you do, then remember that it isn't just a place to have fun in or visit. In our overcrowded island the country is the only place where animals and birds can live a natural life, and for farmers it is a workplace, where they produce food for us all. If you leave gates open, animals will stray and may be involved in road accidents. Litter, besides being unsightly, is dangerous – a plastic bag can kill an animal if it eats it (and they sometimes do), a can or broken bottle can cause a nasty injury. Your dog can injure or even kill farm animals, and if it is caught doing so, the farmer has a legal right to shoot it. So have fun in the country, but remember, and always practise, the Country Code. This is what it says:

> Guard against risk of fire.
> Fasten all gates.
> Keep dogs under proper control.
> Keep to the paths across farm land.
> Avoid damaging fences, hedges and walls.
> Leave no litter.
> Safeguard water supplies.
> Go carefully on country roads.
> Respect the life of the countryside.
> Protect wild life, wild plants and trees.

Physics

Physics is all about lenses, and sound, and electricity, and magnetism, and prisms breaking up light. You will probably do experiments with iron filings and magnets. Don't be tempted to scoop up the iron filings and take them into school dinner to offer to people as black pepper, because you'll ruin their teeth. A good way to cause a diversion is to drop them on the floor so you'll

Did you hear about the cross-eyed teacher?

115

have to spend the rest of the lesson crawling about on your hands and knees trying to pick them up with a magnet. A great deal of confusion can be caused in this way. Similarly, any experiment involving water can be made the excuse for a great deal of mess simply by spilling it (try spilling someone else's after they have carefully measured it out). You will also discover that spring balances make excellent catapults. But you may

She couldn't control her pupils.

be sorry to hear that you can't normally electrocute someone with an electrical experiment as the current isn't strong enough, so bear that in mind before you get any good ideas about how to do away with the school bully.

Cricket

Unless you are one of the *cognoscenti* (if you don't know what that means, look it up in a dictionary – you're supposed to be *learning* something in this book), cricket is a mysterious primeval ritual masquerading as a game. The main points are these. There are two teams. At any one time, one team is batting and the other team is fielding. The fielding team also has to provide various bowlers to throw balls at whichever poor unfortunate member of the batting team has to stand in front of the wicket (the upside-down wooden trident). They will be covered in protective clothing in case the ball smashes its way into some sensitive part of their anatomy. When it is your turn to be batsman you are supposed to try and hit the ball with your bat before it either smashes its way into some sensitive part of *your* anatomy (known as leg before wicket, or lbw) or before it smashes its way into the sensitive parts of the wicket or wooden trident, because if it does that you are out. (Cowards might like to be out first time round because then they don't have to face the ball again.)

If you do manage to hit the ball, then you run towards the opposite wicket, and the person at the opposite wicket runs towards you, and you try and avoid crashing into each other in the middle. The aim is to reach a wicket before one of the other side throws the ball at it, because if they do that you are out too. (It's quite difficult to stay in.) If you've managed to hit the ball a long way away, then you might have to repeat this performance several times, each time being a run, which is what you are supposed to be scoring. If you've managed to hit the ball so hard that it disappears among the spectators, then you can have a rest because you will have automatically scored a four or a six, depending on which way the ball went. The game continues in this haphazard fashion until all the team (usually eleven) is out.

Then it's your turn to field. Unless you are the bowler, in which case you have to run and skip and throw the ball in a special way, you stand around various bits of the field with extraordinary names like 'long leg' and 'silly mid on' waiting until you see a ball that you might possibly be able to catch or retrieve. Some dogs would make much better fielders than humans. If you are right at the edge of the field and nothing much comes your way you might be able to slope off and have tea before the others come in and grab all the sandwiches. This is one of the few advantages of cricket. Another is that the mere attempt to play cricket in England usually makes it rain, in which case you can all go off and have tea anyway.

My Summer Holidays

Make a record of the things you do, week by week.

First week ....

Second week ....

Third week ....

Fourth week...

Fifth week..

Sixth week ....

Any more holiday? ....

We went away on .... (date)

to .... (place)

and stayed at ....

      (name of holiday accommodation)

The most exciting part of the holiday was ....

....

People I met on holiday ....

....

....

(enter their names and addresses
so you can write to them)

The best part of the whole school holiday was ....

....

The worst part of the whole school holiday was ....

....

Quick Reference A–Z

Anything concerned with school not covered in the previous pages will be found in this quick reference section. If it isn't, it's because we ran out of pages!

A

Absence: It is supposed to make the heart grow fonder, but this seldom applies to school. Try not to be absent unless you are really ill. You might miss a lot of fun!

Accuracy: Teachers are very keen on this. If you want to be in their good books then you should try and be keen on it too. If you want to drive them to desperation with your awfulness then try being inaccurate instead.

Activities: You should, for the sake of your fellow pupils, try to join in all these with a good grace. If the strain becomes unbearable, then try hiding in the cloakroom instead.

Apple (for teacher): An apple a day may keep the doctor away, and an onion a day will probably keep everyone away, but taking an apple to your teacher in the hope that it will keep him or her away is a waste of time and money. Much better to eat it yourself.

Why is that little boy kept in a cage in the corner of the room?

B

Blame: Don't blame someone else for something you've done or you'll end up with no friends.

Books: Look after your books and keep them tidy. Cover them with polythene or brown paper to protect them. Don't write in text books, and try to write legibly in exercise books and keep them free from stains from muddy hands, jam, tea, or dripping ice-lollies.

Boys: Boys are noisy, aggressive, rude and pretty nasty, at any rate so it seems if you are a girl. At some magical moment, however, some of the older boys become objects of adoration – also if you're a girl. If you're a boy, you won't have any views about boys because you will think that all other people worthy of consideration are boys anyway.

Brainboxes: A few, a *very* few, pupils can be described as brainboxes. Make sure you sit next to one in every exam or test.

Break: One of the best times of day. Make the most of it and enjoy yourself while you can.

Bullies: Bullies are usually cowards. Keep out of their way, but if this is impossible then stick up for yourself and, if necessary, don't be afraid to get help from fellow pupils or the teacher. Bullies usually disappear quietly when confronted by several people instead of just one.

C

Calculators: Unless you are allowed to use them at school it is best to leave calculators at home. That way you won't lose them or be accused of cheating with them.

Cheating: If you must cheat make sure you're sitting next to someone who is both brainy and has large, clear

That's Egbert. He's the teacher's pet.

handwriting. It's really better not to cheat, though, because you are bound to get caught and be punished.

Christmas pantomime: If your school stages a pantomime you should be in for a good laugh. Pantomimes are meant to be chaotic, and what with the sight of the male teachers running round in football shorts showing their knobbly knees and hairy legs, and the women teachers looking amazing in their mini skirts, you should find plenty to amuse you.

Colds in the head: If you have the kind of cold where you ache all over and your nose is streaming it is best to stay off school, or you'll feel dreadful and give the cold to everyone else. If your cold is just a sniffle, then go to school, but don't cough or sneeze over other people. Use a handkerchief when you sneeze and put your hand in front of your mouth when you cough.

Custard: If you have school dinners avoid the custard at all costs. It is either watery and runny or thick and lumpy.

D

Deafness: A good handicap to cultivate when the teachers are trying to attract your attention or ask you questions. Keep saying, 'Pardon?' – it will drive them mad.

Desk: Try to keep your desk tidy. Don't leave any incriminating evidence in it. Don't write or carve your name on it because you will be found out and made to clean it off or maybe even pay for the damage you've caused.

Dinners: There's more about school dinners on page 24, but this is just a note to say that if you have to eat them, keep the phone number of the local hospital handy. Generally the things to avoid above all are the mashed potatoes, semolina and custard.

Dinner ladies: Always make friends with the dinner ladies. That way, when there is anything edible to eat, you may get a second helping. It could mean the difference between survival and starvation.

Door slamming: This is guaranteed to get you noticed – for all the wrong reasons. It is therefore best avoided.

Dozing: No matter how boring the lesson, try to avoid doing this in class.

E

Eating: One of the most enjoyable ways of spending the time. Teachers don't usually agree, however, so it is best avoided in class.

Education: This is what it's all supposed to be about.

Everything: Don't be everything the teacher expects you to be. If you are, you'll lose all your friends.

Exams: Without a doubt, exams are the worst part of being at school. They are still used as a guide to a pupil's prowess and so it helps in later life to have good results when you are at school. So although it is a ghastly business, it is best to work hard for exams and to try and get good results. That way you won't be made to retake them, which merely makes the awfulness last longer.

Excellence: This, of course, is what every pupil should aim at. But don't just aim at being top of the class and the best in every sport – be excellent at being naughty, too.

F

Fighting: If you must fight, then do it out of sight of the teachers. If you feel you have to kick someone under the desk then make sure the teacher isn't looking. If you come into lessons with a black eye and a bleeding nose, it is difficult to make the teacher believe it had nothing to do with fighting and is merely a result of falling over in the playground.

First day of term: Apart from exams, this day is the worst day of all. After it everything improves. (Mondays feel a bit like this, too.)

Food: When you're at school, try to keep your mind off food, especially towards lunch time and at the end of the afternoon. If you don't you'll never get any work done.

French visits: Some schools are lucky enough to be taken on trips to France. This may be a bit unnerving to the young English boy or girl who doesn't speak the language (despite hours and hours of tuition by despairing teachers). But if you learn the following sentence and remember to keep repeating it while you're over there you should be all right: *'Une glace, s'il vous plaît.'*

TEACHER: What does the word 'unaware' mean?

G

Girls: If you are a boy you will either think that girls are creatures to be adored and worshipped, or a downright nuisance, depending on your age. If you are a girl, you will either like or loathe other girls, depending on what they are like.

H

Handwriting: Teachers always make a point of nagging about pupils' handwriting, but their own is frequently indecipherable. This can sometimes be an advantage, particularly on school reports.

Harassment: Harassment is what supply teachers and first-year pupils are made for, so lose no opportunity to let them know this.

Home time: The best time of any day, when you can have a laugh with your friends, visit the sweet shop and generally lark about. If your teachers are very fussy about you eating in the street, then beware of buying ice-lollies in case they have to be concealed in blazer pockets while the teachers are around. This is not good for either the ice-lolly (ever tried eating an ice-lolly covered in fluff?) or for the blazer (ever tried explaining why there's a horrid sticky mess in your pocket to an irate mum?).

I

Ice-cream: See above – the same applies to ice-creams. When ice-cream is a pudding at school dinner you could try getting a second helping by saying that ––––––– (mention a notorious bully) dropped yours on the floor. It might work.

TESSA: Please, Miss, it's the first thing you put on in the morning.

Idleness: Teachers are always accusing pupils of this. About the only good defence against it is to say you were thinking so hard about the lesson that you hadn't realized you'd been staring out of the window for the last twenty minutes, really you hadn't.

Ink pellets: As you may have read in the section headed *Writing*, on page 75, in the days when desks had ink-wells, soaking little bits of blotting paper in ink and then flicking them across the room with a ruler was a popular pastime (though not with teachers). It is largely obsolete nowadays, but you could try asking your parents if they did it.

Interest: The interest rating of lessons varies greatly. Those that are not very interesting can be made more so by reading a comic under the desk.

J

Jelly: A favourite school dinner pud, jelly can be made to behave in all kinds of unwelcome ways at table. If you like jelly, the best thing to do is to eat it before someone's silly behaviour makes it end up on the floor.

Jewellery: Most schools are not keen on pupils arriving wearing dangly earrings, bracelets, rings and necklaces (and this applies to boys too!). It's not just because they think that school is not the right place to wear jewellery, it is because of the problems caused when items get lost and/or stolen. If you value your jewellery it is best to keep it for special occasions, when you will really appreciate being able to wear it.

Jokes: There are lots of jokes in this book – and not just the obvious ones that appear at the bottom of the page! If you're keen on jokes, try keeping a notebook and

MOTHER: Why do you need to take a ladder to school on your last day?

recording those which people at school (and elsewhere) tell you, so you can remember them and tell them to other people. Otherwise you may forget the punch line, and there's nothing worse than a joke told by someone who can't remember it properly.

July: In most parts of the country this is the best month of the year, for it is the time when exams are over and the long summer holidays start. Hurray for July!

K

Keys: If you are entrusted with keys of any kind don't lose them, drop them down drains, put them in a pocket with a hole in it, leave them behind, or leave them in the lock (unless you have been told to do so).

Kissing: Don't ever indulge in this behind the bike sheds – the head teacher is bound to pass by if you do.

L

Last day at school: One day in the future will be your very last day at school. You may not be able to imagine it, but it will come. It's a funny feeling, for though you may have been longing for it for many years, when it does arrive you may not find it quite as much fun as you had expected. Bear that in mind when it seems much too far off!

Library: A very good place in which to while away the time. Never mind if you can't find the book you want, have a browse through some of the others. You will probably discover the most amazing facts and have a thoroughly enjoyable time.

Litter: Don't drop litter in the streets, the school corridors or anywhere else. Put the bits of paper, sweet

CECIL: Because at the end of it we're off on our climbing holiday.

wrappings, etc., in your pocket until you find a rubbish bin. If the litter is a sticky drinks can, wrap it in a paper hanky or a bag so it doesn't make a mess of your pocket. There is absolutely no excuse for dropping litter, and it makes life unpleasant for everyone, including you.

Love: Never fall in love with a teacher. They're too old for you and not worthy of your devotion.

Lunch times: Apart from being the second best time of day, lunch times can be very useful for catching up on the homework you should have done the previous evening.

M

Mothers: Mothers can fuss an awful lot about what goes on at school, so don't tell them about the most hair-raising episodes.

N

New pupils: There are lots of rituals involving new pupils, most of which are not very kind. While a bit of teasing does no harm, try not to be too horrible. It's bad enough being new at a school without someone being beastly to you as well.

O

Out of school: When I was at school we were always told never to behave in such a way as to dishonour our school uniforms. This didn't worry us – we simply changed out of our uniforms as quickly as possible in any case.

P

Pets, school: If you are in charge of the school pets, be kind to them. They probably don't like being cooped up at school any more than you do. Always make sure they have fresh water to drink, enough food to eat and that their cages are kept clean. All animals need peace and quiet, too, just like you, so don't pester them too much. And remember they need looking after every single day, whether it's a school day or not.

Pets, teachers': Loathed by everyone except the teachers themselves, teachers' pets almost always invite trouble from other pupils. Try tripping one up as he or she rushes eagerly to carry something for the teacher, or, on the odd occasion you *do* know the answer to a question, putting your hand up first. Really awful teachers' pets can be useful subjects for practical jokes (see pages 15, 17, 31, 57, 81, 82, 91).

Playground: Hurray for playgrounds, where you can get away from teachers and do as you like. If yours has any useful corners you can try hiding round them when the bell goes in the hope that you won't be discovered. Later, say you'd gone to the lavatory and didn't hear the bell.

Poker face: A poker face is one absolutely devoid of expression. The term comes from the card game poker, in which players do their utmost not to let their fellows know by their expression whether they have a good hand of cards or not. It is a useful trick to cultivate for those occasions on which *someone* is accused of doing something. Those who know anything about the misdemeanour are asked to tell all. If you can keep this expressionless face up then you will not give away that you know very well that Sally Jones did it, Anne had a hand in it, and you were the look-out.

PT: PT stands for Physical Torture. It makes your legs ache, your arms ache, and generally leaves you feeling like a piece of wet string. And it's called keeping fit!

Punishment: Punishment is something that should never happen to you. You are only punished if you are caught – and if you are caught then you have failed in whatever naughtiness you were up to!

Fortunately, for most people, the days of caning and being rapped over the knuckles with a ruler have gone – but punishment can still be pretty dreary. Having to stay in after school and write lines (even if you are clever enough to use two or even three pens at once), or having to give up your break or lunch time to do work that should have been done the night before is no fun and not really worth it. Better to get the work done at the right time!

Some teachers, who consider they have a sense of humour, have particularly eccentric forms of punishing pupils. You may have one in your school whose favourite idea is to make you stand on a chair with your hands on your head and not move for an hour. If you've ever done it you'll know it's a lot worse than it sounds!

So do try to avoid being punished – either by being so clever in your naughtiness that you get away with it, or, if you can't do that, by behaving so well that no one would ever think of punishing you!

Q

Questions: It's usually the teachers who ask the questions, but you could try asking a few yourself. Say you are in a physics lesson and told 'light travels in straight lines'. Ask why. If you are then told because that is the way it behaves, ask why again. Your teacher will be unable to answer the questions and will probably get hot and bothered. He/she may also get cross with you, and *before* this happens is the time to stop.

Queues: The British are supposed to like queuing for things, so if you have to form a queue make it a nice orderly one and don't try to sneak in. The chances are that someone will retaliate if you do, anyway, especially if they've been there a long time.

R

The three Rs: Reading, writing and arithmetic – the three Rs – are supposed to be the backbone of education. But the man who coined the phrase, Sir William Curtis, was illiterate. He could neither read nor write.

Reasons: Reasons are excuses that sound plausible.

Right and wrong: You are supposed to know the difference between these before you go to school, though on some occasions it's more complicated than on others. If in doubt, try asking why certain things are considered right and others considered wrong – you will be able to get an adult very confused.

S

School choir: This is another name for a collection of people who can produce a noise like a horde of cats on a moonlit night, apparently without effort.

Sign language: Before exams and other important events when you will not be allowed to speak to your friends in class, invent a simple sign language and teach it to all your friends. It can consist of undetectable signs such as blowing your nose, coughing, scratching your head or an ear, playing with your hair or collar as if deep in thought, and so on. For example, in an exam, scratching the head might mean 'How are you getting on?', which could be answered by pulling at an ear, for 'OK', or rubbing the end of your nose, for 'very badly'.

T

Trespassing: If you are a girl at an all-girls' school, this is the name the teachers give to boys caught on the premises trying to visit their girlfriends.

U

U-turn: This is what you should do when you see a teacher advancing towards you.

University: If you are in the secondary school, always tell the teachers that you are aiming to go to university, even if you are not, because then they will feel that you are clever and might treat you better. You might be able to fool some of them for quite a long time with this ploy.

V

Viva voce: This is an oral examination – something you will have towards GCSE-time if you study foreign languages. The examiner will converse with you in the language and ask you questions. It is rarely an enjoyable experience!

W

Worship, acts of: If yours is a church school you will know what this means. If it isn't, it means going to church or having a religious service at school. It can be a good time for catching up on sleep, and the time spent bending over saying prayers is useful for exchanging gossip or sweets.

X

eXcitement: The exciting times at school tend to be just before breaking up for holidays and half terms. If you feel the rest of the year is a bit lacking in excitement, you could try one of the following:

Selling the school to a rich tourist.
Elaborate hoaxes such as organising the cloakroom facilities on a mock-timetable basis.
Arranging for a demolition contractor to come round and start dismantling the school.
Putting up a notice to the effect that the school has been closed until further notice owing to an outbreak of foot-and-mouth disease.

Y

Yawning: Many teachers take yawning in their lessons as a personal insult, so do it a lot if you want to annoy them, but control yourself if you are already in their bad books.

Z

Zoo: Where all the teachers and quite a lot of the pupils rightfully belong.

MY RECORD BOOK

GYLES BRANDRETH

The pogo bouncing, baked bean picking, wellie-wanging, jolly jelly record book!

How many pairs of socks can *you* put on, one on top of another? Can *you* eat an entire tin of baked beans in 19 minutes using only a cocktail stick? And what exactly *are* the credentials for being a record-breaker?

YOU'D BETTER GET A COPY AT RECORD SPEED AND FIND OUT!

KNIGHT BOOKS

DIRTY, LOUD AND BRILLIANT

CAROL VORDERMAN

Bet you can't
*hold a cup with one finger
*light a torch with a lemon
*make a table top hovercraft
With DIRTY, LOUD AND BRILLIANT – you can!

Masses of easy-to-follow mind-boggling experiments using stuff you'll find at home.

Have a Dirty, Loud and Brilliant time!

KNIGHT BOOKS

THE RAINY DAY SURVIVAL BOOK

JEREMY TAPSCOTT

This book is here to save you. Packed with 1001 cheap, easy and fun things to do — not just on rainy days but during thunderstorms and even a monsoon! Simply showered with illustrations and positively downpoured with original ideas.

KNIGHT BOOKS

A CATALOGUE OF COMIC VERSE

COLLECTED AND ILLUSTRATED BY
ROLF HARRIS

A cattle dog (as they say in Australia!) jam-packed with great poems on a variety of different topics – including cats and dogs – to say nothing of tigers and terrified tortoises, some rather curious eating habits and some loony relations.

This rumbustious collection for children of all ages has been compiled and interpreted with wittily refreshing drawings by Rolf Harris, author of the best-selling *Your Cartoon Time*, and favourite of children everywhere.

KNIGHT BOOKS

MY DIARY

GYLES BRANDRETH

Can your diary make you laugh, get you fit and bowl you over with facts? Can it suggest cunning practical jokes, pose baffling brain-teasers and give you fun ideas for your spare time? And *on top of all this* does it give you everything you would expect from a diary?

My Diary has it all; it's the ultimate diary and it's your chance for the most exciting year ever!

KNIGHT BOOKS

ODYSSEUS
THE GREATEST HERO OF THEM ALL

TONY ROBINSON AND RICHARD CURTIS

'They were all standing in a circle in the middle of the room; the most powerful men in the world all together. Drawing their daggers, they cut their right hands, and as the blood dripped on to the pile of gold, they swore Odysseus' vow: Helen could marry whom she liked, and the Princes would defend them both. There was a silence, broken only by the drip of red blood on gold.'

Everyone's heard of the wooden horse of Troy, haven't they? And everyone knows of the beauty of Helen — whose face once launched a thousand ships — don't they? Well this is the story the way Odysseus saw it all, from his boyhood to his participation in the bloody Trojan war itself.

Based on the exciting and award-winning BBC TV series.

KNIGHT BOOKS

YOUR CARTOON TIME

ROLF HARRIS

Did you know that you can draw?

Rolf Harris shows you how — clearly and simply — in *Your Cartoon Time*. Starting with stick figures, he explains how to develop these step-by-step into your own stylish characters, and there are ideas too for how you can use your drawings — as birthday cards, home movies and so on.

Drawing is fun!

All you need is a pencil, paper and Rolf Harris's book — *Your Cartoon Time*.

KNIGHT BOOKS